ORIENTAL GLAZES

Northwest Vista College
Learning Resource Center
3535 North Ellison Drive
San Antonio, Texas 78251

D1520216

OTHER TITLES IN THE SERIES

ORIENTAL
GLAZES

Michael Bailey

A&C Black • London

University of Pennsylvania • Philadelphia

For Jan, Jo and Judy

First published in Great Britain in 2004
A & C Black Publishers Limited
Alderman House, 37 Soho Square
London W1D 3QZ
www.acblack.com

ISBN 0-7136-6214-X

Published simultaneously in the USA by
University of Pennsylvania Press
4200 Pine Street, Philadelphia,
Pennsylvania 19104-4011

ISBN 0-8122-1890-6

CIP Catalogue records for this book are available from
the British Library and the U.S. Library of Congress.

Michael Bailey has asserted his right under the
Copyright, Design and Patents Act, 1988, to be
identified as the author of this work.

Book design by Susan McIntyre
Cover design by Dorothy Moir

Cover illustrations (front): Large vase by David Frith
using COPR 11 (see p.103).
Cover illustration (back): Bowl by Malcolm Jepson
using JUN 6.
Frontispiece: Copper red teapot by Melanie Brown
using COPR 5 (see p.98).

Printed in China by WKT Company Ltd.

A & C Black uses paper produced with elemental
chlorine-free pulp, harvested from managed
sustainable forests.

Contents

Acknowledgements

My warm and heartfelt thanks go to: Jan, and the rest of the family for their forbearance whilst I indulge in my various hobbies; my editors, Linda Lambert and Alison Stace, for all their help and encouragement; the contributors – Roger Brann, John Britt, Melanie Brown, Mike Dodd, David Frith, Margaret Frith, Michael Gaitskell, Liz Gale, Paul Green, John Harlow, Glyn and Vic Harris, Joanna Howells, Malcolm Jepson, Richard Kelham, John Leach, 'Made in Cley', Christine McColl, David and Simone McDowell, Mark Melbourne, Steve Mills, Christine and Peter Penfold, Douglas Phillips, Chris Prindl, Jim Robison, Phil Rogers, Marcia Selsor, Brian Simmons, Paul Stubbs, Matthew Waite and David Winkley, for generously providing notes, glaze recipes, pots to photograph and slides; my partners, Kate and Steve Mills at Bath Potters' Supplies, for their flexibility, support and tolerance; Nick Stokes for help in mixing up some of the glaze tests; John Harlow and Paul Stubbs for firing all of the test tiles; David Hewitt for allowing the use of his 'CeramDat' computer program to calculate glaze analyses, plus much valued help with research and the interchange of ideas.

And finally I must thank Nigel Wood who wrote *Oriental Glazes: their Chemistry, Origins and Re-creation*. This was published in 1978 in the Ceramic Skillbooks series and is one of the best books I have ever read. I feel very honoured in being allowed to re-cycle *Oriental Glazes* as the title for this book.

Chapter One
Introduction

This book is a sequel to *Glazes Cone 6* (also in this Ceramics Handbook series), which looks at oxidised glazes for firing in an electric kiln. Here, in *Oriental Glazes*, the emphasis is on firing in a flame kiln (using gas, oil, propane or wood), with the oxygen supply restricted at the top end of the firing. This creates the reducing effect that brings about the changes, especially to the metallic colouring oxides copper and iron, that produce the subtle and beautiful qualities associated with the classic Far Eastern glazes.

However, as a book it must also stand in its own right and it has been necessary to restate a very helpful way of thinking about glazes – that is, by looking at their chemical composition and plotting them graphically (see below). This can be useful diagnostically:
a) To get an idea as to how a glaze will behave.
b) The direction that might be taken should a glaze need to be altered.

This not only shows how the various glaze types relate to one other, but can also indicate the direction that one might take to find a specific glaze. In fact this idea can even be extended to include the glaze-making raw materials (see p.110). By similarly plotting them on the graph we can begin to make much better decisions about which materials to use.

To help develop this idea the glazes are separated into three main areas:
1. The chapter on low iron glazes takes

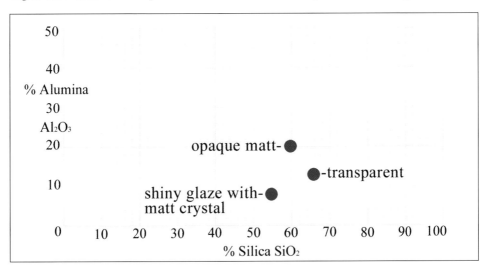

(**Fig. 1**) Plotting glazes on a graph.

these transparent, shiny glazes as a starting point and explores the ways that such 'perfect' glazes can be 'unbalanced' to produce satin and matt surfaces.

2. The chapter on high iron glazes investigates the relationship between shiny black tenmokus, brown 'ash' glazes, hare's fur, iron reds, kakis, oil-spots and tea-dusts.

3. The chapter on copper glazes explains how producing reds, greens and blues depends upon the firing conditions and glaze ingredients used.

For comparison and consistency the glazes are organised as base recipes with the ingredients listed as a percentage correct to one decimal place, and their analyses correct to two decimal places. The ingredients, too, for ease of comparison, are listed in the order: feldspars, clays, frits, fluxes and finally silica (flint or quartz). The colouring and opacifying oxides are listed as a percentage additional to the base glaze. The glaze number/reference system consists of using the first three letters of the glaze type e.g. CEL1 for celadon glaze Number 1, or ORA1 for orange red glaze Number 1, etc. These are then numbered sequentially as they appear in each chapter and enable the recipe to be related to the illustrations and any relevant text. The firing range for each recipe is given as a cone number. This is explained in greater detail on pp.19–20.

A chapter about kilns and firing has been included. Compared with electric kilns, flame kilns do need a raised level of commitment. As a general rule it is much easier and far less time-consuming to fire an electric kiln. Indeed, with the aid of simple programmers they actually fire themselves! With a flame kiln the potter has to be more on hand throughout the firing, balancing the fuel and air as a means of controlling the temperature rise and the atmosphere. Setting the reduction at the correct time is critical and missing this 'window of opportunity' can ruin a lot of work. However, reduction firing produces that extra quality that seems impossible to achieve in an electric kiln and clearly, despite the extra work, many potters and sculptors think that it is worth doing.

Please remember that there are many variables in making, glazing and firing pottery. Obviously the glaze recipe is a good starting point but other significant factors include:

- The underlying clay body or slip
- The bisque firing temperature
- Porosity of the bisque
- How much water to add to the glaze – its specific gravity
- Glaze thickness (dipping time)
- The temperature/heat-work needed to melt the glaze
- The cooling rate
- The kiln atmosphere (including when to reduce)
- The geological origin of the glaze ingredients
- Whether fired on a flat or a vertical surface
- In illustrating glazes – the photographic processes
- In calculating glazes – different analyses for the same material

All, or some, of these may conspire to make your glazes come out slightly differently to the ones shown here.

Chapter Two
Making glazes

Glazing is about putting a coating of glass onto a piece of clay. The first step is to find some way of applying this glaze coat to the work; the second step is the province of the pyro-enthusiast – heating it up until it melts. These two steps may even be combined and it is possible to glaze pots within the kiln as part of the firing process.

The applied glaze

In the main, though, the glazes that we are dealing with will be applied to the clay as a thin coat before it goes into the kiln (as opposed to salt- or some wood-firing in which the sodium vapours or wood ash settle on the pots in the kiln). The usual way is to mix the glaze ingredients with water to the consistency of a thin cream. This is then passed through a sieve, which breaks up any lumps and removes any coarse particles. Most potters would use at least an 80s-mesh sieve; i.e. 80 holes to the inch, although some go as fine as a 200s mesh.

The glaze can either be applied by dipping the work in the glaze, or by painting or spraying the glaze onto the ware. The materials need to be finely powdered as this helps the glaze ingredients stay in suspension. It also provides a greater surface contact between the particles, aiding melting during the firing.

Glaze preparation: Steve Mills sieving a glaze.

Steve Mills dipping a pot to get an even application of glaze before firing.

The glaze-making materials

In one way or another all of the glaze-making ingredients will have come from minerals in the earth's crust. Fortunately for the glaze maker, some geological and even biological processes have produced enormous quantities of fairly homogeneous deposits and these can be mined on an industrial scale. This has benefits both in terms of keeping the cost of finely milled materials down and in employing experts to test and, if necessary, blend to produce a consistent product. (Not that this should stop potters from collecting their own glaze materials.)

All glazes are based on a combination of three components: fluxes, stabilisers and glass formers.

The Fluxes

As the name implies, fluxes bring about flow and help the glaze to melt. The most powerful fluxes are the alkalis:

Oxide	Chemical symbol	Example of mineral providing this chemical
Potassium oxide	K_2O	Potash feldspar
Sodium oxide	Na_2O	Soda feldspar
Lithium oxide	Li_2O	Lithium carbonate

The other fluxes are the alkaline earths. These are less reactive, especially at lower temperatures in the earthenware range (up to 1150°C/2102°F). They are, however, very important, imparting greater stability and assisting glaze fit.

Oxide	Chemical symbol	Examples of minerals providing this chemical
Calcium oxide	CaO	Limestone, whiting
Magnesium oxide	MgO	Magnesium carbonate, talc
Barium oxide	BaO	Barium carbonate
Zinc oxide	ZnO	Zinc oxide

The Stabilisers

The main stabiliser in glazes is alumina (Al_2O_3). This is typically introduced into the glaze as a clay but it is also inevitably introduced as part of the chemical make-up of feldspar.

Glass formers

By far the most important glass former is silica (SiO_2). It can be added directly to the glaze as flint or quartz; ingredients which are virtually 100% pure SiO_2. However, silica may also be introduced as part of the chemical composition of other more complex minerals – the main ones being clays, feldspars, talc, wollastonite and wood ash. P_2O_5 phosphorous pentoxide and TiO_2 are possible routes for the formation of the opalescent Jun glazes. Boric oxide (B_2O_3) is difficult to classify. It behaves as a glass former but melts at a low temperature, consequently acting as a flux, yet is logically classed as a stabiliser alongside Al_2O_3.

On their own many of the materials that are melted to form a glaze will be quite unpromising. For example, opposite are three button tests showing whiting (i.e. calcium carbonate), china clay and quartz fired to cone 9. Button tests are quick to do. The material is simply mixed with water into a thin paste (a cup and spoon are all that is needed). The spoon can then be used to scoop and smear the paste onto a tile, ideally spreading it to show thin, medium (1–2 mm) and thick areas (3 mm).

Individually these materials show very little inclination to melt at this temperature but together, when combined in just the right proportions, they can make the glaze on the centre tile. Juggling the flux, stabiliser and glass former is a central theme of this book.

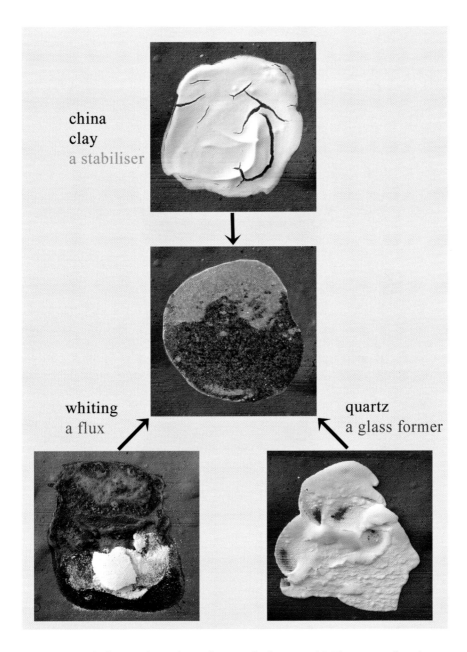

Button tests of whiting, china clay and quartz fired to cone 10. The centre tile is the glaze produced from an equal-parts mix of these three materials.

Chapter Three
Using graphs to study glazes

The two main methods used by potters to describe the chemical composition of glazes are the 'unity formula' and the 'percentage analysis', and both systems may be used for plotting the position of glazes on a graph. This type of representation is an extremely helpful device that shows visually how the various glaze types and the glaze-forming minerals relate to one other.

The Unity formula

In the unity formula, the main glaze components are split into their three groups: fluxes, stabilisers and glass formers. The molecular ratio of the fluxes is calculated so that they add up to 1 (hence 'unity') and this is followed by the proportion of the stabilisers and glass formers. As examples, here are two glazes:

An alumina matt cone 9 glaze

Fluxes	Stabiliser	Glass former
0.30 K_2O	0.70 Al_2O_3	3.50 SiO_2
0.70 CaO		
1.00		

A shiny transparent cone 9 glaze

Fluxes	Stabiliser	Glass former
0.25 K_2O	0.35 Al_2O_3	3.20 SiO_2
0.75 CaO		
1.00		

By keeping the fluxes as a constant, it is possible to compare glazes by looking at the amounts of the stabiliser alumina (Al_2O_3) and the glass former silica (SiO_2). Now, with just two variables, we can easily plot these glazes on a graph (see Fig.2).

This is a perfectly good way of graphically representing most glazes which plot out in a manageable area of the graph, and is a method adopted, for example, by Ian Currie in his book *Stoneware Glazes: A Systematic Approach*, and myself in *Glazes Cone 6*. However, this system runs into a major problem if the discussion is expanded to represent raw materials such as clays on the graph. Here, for example, is the unity formula for a china clay:

Fluxes	Stabiliser	Glass former
0.35 K_2O	34.48 Al_2O_3	71.62 SiO_2
0.10 Na_2O		
0.31 CaO		
0.24 MgO		
1.00		

To give this china clay a position, and keep to the same scale as in Fig. 2, we would need a piece of graph paper approximately 2.5 m (8 ft) high and 3 m (10 ft) wide! Indeed, in this system, it is impossible to represent materials such as pure alumina or silica on the graph, as neither of these materials possess any fluxes and cannot therefore be manipulated mathematically into a unity formula. We could resort to log scales on each axis, or use a triaxial graph, but then we lose the advantage of the simplicity of this straightforward approach.

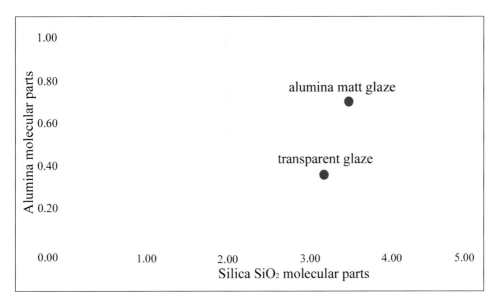

(**Fig. 2**) Example of plotting two glazes based on the unity formula. An alumina matt glaze at 0.7 Al_2O_3:3.50 SiO_2. A shiny transparent glaze at 0.35 Al_2O_3:3.20 SiO_2.

The percentage analysis

The percentage analysis, sometimes called the ultimate analysis, gives the actual weight of the oxides in the fired glaze. The two glazes given as examples for plotting out in the unity formula would be written as:

% analysis of an alumina matt cone 9 glaze
SiO_2 60.21; Al_2O_3 20.47 CaO 11.24; K_2O 8.08

% analysis of a transparent shiny cone 9 glaze
SiO_2 65.48; Al_2O_3 12.18 CaO 14.32; K_2O 8.02

Their alumina Al_2O_3: silica SiO_2 ratio can be plotted in a similar way:
The alumina matt glaze position is at Al_2O_3 20.47%: SiO_2 60.21% and the transparent glaze position is at Al_2O_3 12.18%: SiO_2 65.48% (see Fig. 3).

The one big advantage of using the percentage analysis graph is that all the raw materials used in making glazes can also be given positions on the graph. The china clay, that gave such a problem when we tried to plot its position with a unity formula, has a percentage analysis of:

% analysis of a china clay
SiO_2 53.87; Al_2O_3 45.20 CaO 0.30; MgO 0.12; K_2O 0.41; Na_2O 0.10

This, too, can now be added to the graph (Fig. 3) so that this particular china clay's position is at Al_2O_3 45.20%:SiO_2 53.87%.

A few other glaze ingredients have also been added to the graph to illustrate this system in use. This is the main reason for adopting the percentage analysis system throughout the book; the relevance of this will hopefully become apparent in later chapters!

13

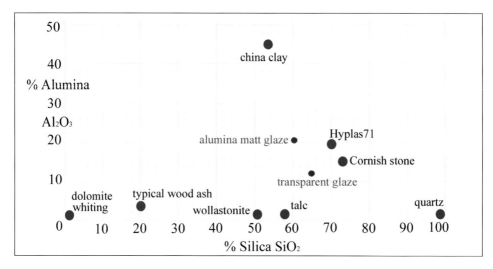

(**Fig. 3**) Example of plotting the alumina Al_2O_3:silica SiO_2 ratio based on the percentage analysis for an alumina matt glaze (red dot), a transparent glaze (red dot), and various raw materials (blue dots).

Chapter Four
Kilns and firing

After analysing a questionnaire sent out to the contributors of this book, it soon became apparent that there is considerable variation in the types of kiln and firing regimes used by reduction firing potters. Propane is used for fuel by 50% followed by 25% using oil, with the remainder equally divided between natural gas and wood.

Firing times also varied greatly from as little as 5 hours to as long as 50 hours, but these were atypical and most potters fired in 12 to 16 hours (average 14.5 hours). Around one third raw glaze – that is the work is glazed at the leather-hard to dry stage. The big advantage of this single firing method is that the packing and unpacking at the bisque stage are eliminated. (We won't mention the problems for the moment.)

Only one potter had bought a purpose-built kiln. One had cannibalised a large old electric kiln by removing the elements and fitting burners and flues. Everyone else had built their own, the majority using lightweight insulating bricks. How to build a kiln is outside the scope of the book but there are several reference works that should be helpful (see Bibliography on p.127). A good way to find out how to build a kiln is to visit a potter who has one that you can copy Fortunately nearly all potters, especially potters that do reduction firing, are for some inexplicable reason really nice, helpful people and are often prepared to give advice. It makes the job of building

one much easier if you can take the measurements from an existing kiln and find out where to buy all the bits and pieces. The main thing is not to be scared of doing so. Providing that you are capable, competent, logical, practical, pragmatic, proficient and sensible (if not, don't attempt becoming a reduction firing potter) then building your own kiln is a realistic option.

The choice of kiln size varied from 0.1 m³ to 4 m³ (4 cu. ft to 120 cu. ft) but it was noticeable that a majority had kilns around 1 m³ (34 cu ft). Given that it actually takes very little more time and effort to fire a 1.6 m³ (60 cu. ft) than a 0.3 m³ (12 cu. ft) kiln, the choice of kiln size comes down to how frequently you want to fire. This can be an important question as it determines one's whole making, glazing and firing cycle.

Natural gas, propane and oil kilns

In many respects these kilns are quite similar as they all use hydrocarbons – fuels which were once tropical forests. In burning them we are completing the decomposition and releasing the sun's energy and the CO_2 that was stored up by photosynthesis many millions of years ago. The flame is introduced into the kiln through a hole called a 'quarl', by a burner that is constructed to combine the fuel and the primary air. Additional secondary air is usually drawn into the kiln by the pull of the chimney, but a few kilns are fan-assisted. The concentrated nature of the fuel means that the fireboxes can be fairly small, at least in comparison with wood kilns. Oil, which still has to be vaporised, needs a larger firebox than gas. Chimneys on propane kilns usually only need to be the same height as the kiln, whereas for natural gas and oil kilns they need to be taller – around three times the height of the kiln chamber.

Wood kilns

Wood-fired kilns are in a class of their own. They need large fireboxes and a large supply of clean, dry wood. A few expert friends to help with the stoking doesn't go amiss either. Some potters use gas or oil for preheating and the early stages of the firing, and introduce wood when it is time to start reducing, although to some this conflicts with their philosophy and the spirit behind the process.

An attraction of electric kilns is the low cost of control mechanisms. Indeed many are fully automatic, with the kiln's programmer providing staged temperature increases, a timed soak at top temperature and even the ability to control the rate of cooling. Nothing like this is available if you want to do reduction firing in a flame kiln; at least not within the budget of any of my potting friends and acquaintances. Nor, I suspect, would they want it to be. The way the pots are fired makes a vital contribution, and is inextricably linked to their final appearance. In electing to make reduction-fired pots, the potter takes on the firing of the kiln as an integral part of the process.

Reduction firing

In reduction firing some time has to be spent starving the kiln of oxygen. The way that this is achieved will depend upon the fuel and kiln design. The timing and strength of reduction will also vary as particular clays and glaze effects need different treatments. The following three descriptions have been chosen to illustrate something of the various approaches, and to explain the key stages in the reduction firing process. It should be stated though that there is never a total consensus about how a kiln should be fired!

A fast firing

This is based on a 7½-hour glaze firing (see Fig.4) of small to medium sized wheel-thrown pots (mugs, jugs, teapots, etc.) in a fast-firing 0.1m³ (4 cu. ft) propane gas kiln to cone 10. (The pots have been bisque fired to 1020°C/1868°F/cone 06 and then glazed a few days before the firing.)

1. 0°C – 150°C (32°F – 302°F) in 1 hour to dry out water absorbed by the body during glazing.
2. 150°C – 970°C (302°F – 1778°F) in 3 hours. A clean oxidising setting of the fire until cone 07 begins to bend.
3. 970°C – 1000°C (1778°F – 1832°F) for 30 minutes. Fairly heavy reduction to reduce the iron in the clay. The fuel setting is not changed and the reduction is created by cutting down on the pull of the chimney. This may be done by:
   a. Pushing a damper plate part way into the base of the chimney.
   b. Sliding a brick or kiln shelf partly across the top of the chimney.
   c. Taking a brick (or bricks) out of the base of the chimney.

Whichever system is employed the net effect is to decrease the amount of secondary air being drawn into the firebox. The temperature may even stick at this point as the fuel is now being burnt inefficiently. There may be a slightly sulphurous smell in the air and if the spyhole brick is briefly removed, a 10 cm (4 in.) flame licks out. The aim at this stage is to reduce the iron in the clay body before the glaze starts to melt.

4. 1000°C – 1220°C (1832°F – 2228°F) in 2 hours. The pull of the chimney is increased slightly, e.g. by easing open the damper by 1–2 mm (⅟₁₆ in.). The kiln is kept in reduction, but this is a lighter reduction, allowing the temperature to rise. There may come a point when the temperature will not increase without losing reduction. In this case it will be necessary to slightly increase the fuel (so that the kiln is reducing too heavily) and then get back to a light/medium reduction by increasing the pull of the chimney. Cone 8 starts to bend.

5. 1220°C – 1260°C (2228°F – 2300°F) in 1 hour. Light reduction/neutral atmosphere. Really a soaking period in which cone 9 and 10 gradually go over. Kiln turned off when cone 10 has gone point down; cone 11 has started to bend.

6. Burner ports and chimney closed up. Some potters do this immediately, quite a few let the temperature drop to 1000°C (1832°F) before closing, and a few others will let the temperature drop even further to 750°C (1382°F) before clamming up. The cooling rate can have a significant effect on the final appearance of certain glazes. A fast cool aids transparent glazes, whereas slow cooling can promote opacity due to crystal growth.

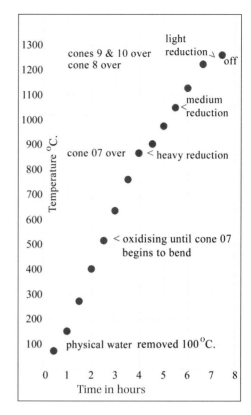

(Fig. 4) Time/temperature graph for a fast firing in a small kiln. Oxidising (blue dots), reducing (red dots).

A copper red glaze firing

This is based on the same fast-firing 0.1 m³ (4 cu. ft) propane gas kiln, but with the intention of producing copper red glazes. The pots have been bisque fired to 1020°C/1868°F (cone 06), with a 1 hour soak, and then glazed a few days before the firing.

1. 0°C – 150°C (32°F – 302°F) in 1 hour to dry out the water absorbed by the body during glazing.
2. 150°C – 850°C (302°F – 1562°F) in 3 hours. A clean oxidising setting of the fire.
3. 850°C – 900°C (1562°F – 1652°F)

for 30 minutes. Heavy reduction to reduce the copper in the glaze.

4. 900°C – 1220°C (1652°F – 2228°F) in 4 hours. The pull of the chimney is increased slightly but medium reduction is maintained. Cone 8 starts to bend.

5. 1220°C – 1250°C (2228°F – 2282°F) in 1½ hours. Medium reduction, cone 9 and 10 gradually go over. Kiln turned off when cone 10 has gone point down, cone 11 has started to bend.

6. Burner ports and chimney kept open for 30 minutes allowing a rapid cool to 900°C (1652°F) before closing.

Total firing time 10½ hours.

Raw firing

This is a fairly cautious regime based on a raw-glaze firing of small, medium and large wheel-thrown pots (mugs, casseroles, breadcrocks, etc.) in a 0.75 m³ (27 cu. ft) kiln gas kiln to cone 10. The pots have been glazed a few days before the firing. One may well go faster or slower than the times suggested here – so much depends on the thickness of the ware and the openness of the clay body (see Fig. 5).

1. Preheating (possibly up to 8 hours). This may be done during the day, or the evening before the firing starts. The idea is to get the pots as dry as possible and in some cases dry out the kiln bricks too.

2. 0°C – 150°C (32 – 302°F) in 3 hours. Only one burner on. A low 'candle' flame and a very slow rise through the 100°C (212°F) barrier to drive off the water of plasticity. The change of phase from a liquid to a gas of even a tiny residue of water remaining within

the clay can be enough to blow the work apart. The force of the explosion is usually enough to send tiny bits of clay into all areas of the kiln. If a dull-sounding thud is heard, it is best to stop the firing, clean up, repack and start again.

3. 150°C – 450°C (302°F – 842°F) in 3 hours. Second burner lit, keeping a clean oxidising setting of the fire. The chemical water is driven off at around 600°C (1112°F).

4. 450°C – 850°C (842°F – 1562°F) in 4 hours. Oxidising flame, the temperature can be allowed to rise more rapidly.

5. 850°C – 970°C (1562°F – 1778°F) in 2 hours. An oxidising flame. This is a tricky period for raw glazers. The firing is slowed down to allow time for any carbonates and sulphates in the clay to burn out, otherwise they cause bloating (raised blisters in the clay) later in the firing.

6. 970°C – 1000°C (1778°F – 1832°F) in 1 hour. Fairly heavy reduction to reduce the iron in the clay. The temperature may even stick at this point. The 850° – 1040°C (1562° – 1904°F) stage can be a problem with certain clays and glazes. The aim is to burn out any carbonates and sulphates in the clay and then reduce the iron in the clay body before the glaze starts to melt. This will be a matter of trial and error. Bloating may be cured by extending the clean burning time around 900°C (1652°F). Under-reduced clay, usually noticed just above the firebox, can be cured by starting the reduction earlier. It is also worth checking that the burners are balanced and that one firebox is not getting hotter than the other. If starting to experiment with raw glazing, it is advisable to try as many clay/glaze combinations as possible. Some clays

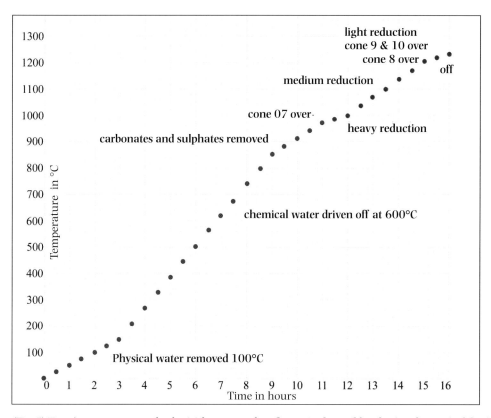

(Fig. 5) Time/temperature graph of a 16-hour raw-glaze firing. Oxidising (blue dots), reducing (red dots).

are definitely much better for raw glazing than others.

7. 1000° – 1200°C (1832° – 2192°F) in 3 hours. The kiln is kept in reduction but this is a lighter reduction allowing the temperature to gradually rise. Cone 8 starts to bend.

8. 1200° – 1230°C (2192° – 2246°F) in 1 hour. Light reduction/ neutral atmosphere. Really a soaking period in which cones 9 and 10 gradually go over. Kiln turned off when cone 10 has gone point down, cone 11 starting to bend.

9. Burner ports and chimney closed up. See the discussion about when to clam up in the previous description of fast firing (see p.17).

Typical firing time (excluding the preheating) 16–17 hours.

Pyrometry

The three main devices used by potters for observing the progress of a firing are cones, draw trials and pyrometers. An oxygen-probe can be used to monitor the kiln atmosphere.

Cones

The glaze recipes in this book use a cone reference to indicate their firing range. For example, TRA 1 Transparent cone 8–10 means that the glaze should work if it is fired in a kiln that has got hot enough to cause either cone 8, 9 or 10

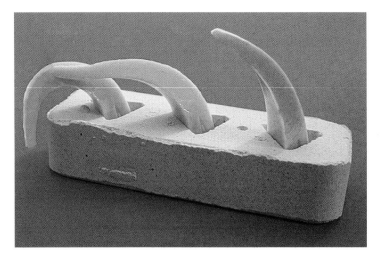

to start melting, i.e., bending over to form an arch. Most of the potters who do reduction firing use cones as the final arbiter in judging when a kiln should be shut down. This is not surprising as the cones, which measure heat-work, are affected by the same factors of time and temperature that affect the melting of glazes (see pp.125–6 for cone chart). Cones, however, cease to be accurate if used in salt kilns or in the type of wood-fired kiln that deposits wood ash on the ware. These deposits have a fluxing effect on the cones, causing them to bend prematurely.

Draw trials

With draw trials, the idea is to hook out pieces of fired/glazed clay towards the end of the firing, usually with an appropriate iron rod. They are mainly used by salt- and some wood-firers to judge the formation of a glaze coating by the build up of sodium vapour or wood ash deposits. They can also be used to assess how applied glazes are melting. (Indeed, there is a theory that raku pottery began as little draw-trial bowls removed from the kiln towards the end of the firing.) In practice, a draw trial looks quite different

to the work that has remained in the kiln and cooled down slowly. However, a very useful reference collection can be built up in which the appearance of a draw trial can be related to the fired work.

Pyrometers

Pyrometers measure temperature and consist of a thermocouple, a meter and a compensating cable to connect them together. Ideally, the end of the thermocouple probe needs to project about 5 cm

Example of a draw trial used to assess glaze melt.

20

(2 in.) into the kiln. The ceramic sheath is thin and easily broken, so the choice of position in the kiln may need some thought – keeping it out of harm's way and yet giving a representative reading. There is a choice of two types of meter: 'analogue' or 'digital'. The analogue has an arm that moves across a Fahrenheit or Celsius calibrated scale. The advantage of analogues is that they don't need batteries, but on the debit side they are less accurate, and the small scale gives a less precise reading. Digital pyrometers, on the other hand, do give precise readings. This is a great help in the latter part of the firing when one can see, within a few minutes, whether the temperature is actually going up or down or remaining stationary. Because pyrometers give a continuous reading the potter can keep a 'kiln log book', by recording temperature against time and taking notes about how the kiln is controlled, with little sketches added to show how the cones are bending. These records are very useful, especially as one gets to know a kiln, and a great help in identifying where improvements might be made to subsequent firings, or even, when the happy day comes, repeating a good one.

Oxygen-probes

These sample the atmosphere in the kiln and can greatly increase the efficiency, as well as one's understanding, of the firing process. The most efficient use of the fuel is a setting that is on the cusp of going from an oxidising to a neutral atmosphere. The further the kiln atmosphere moves to either side of this position, either reducing or oxidising, the more inefficient the firing becomes.

Reducing atmospheres are, of course, inefficient because the kiln is starved of oxygen and up to a point this is an accepted part of the firing process. However, reducing too heavily is needlessly wasteful and an oxygen-probe can help check this.

The other side of this efficiency line is an excess of air. In this scenario, firing with the chimney and all ports open means that too much cold, secondary air is being drawn into the kiln. For example, I have a friend who does oxidised earthenware and is really worried about accidentally creating a reducing atmosphere. By borrowing an oxygen analyser it was possible to demonstrate that the chimney exit could be closed down to a considerable extent before the kiln would start to reduce; which meant a substantial saving on the fuel bill.

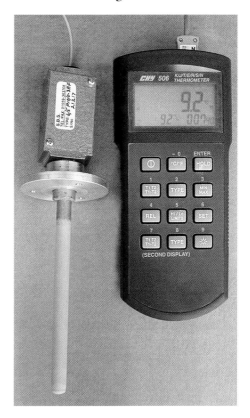

Digital pyrometer and thermouple.

Chapter Five
The low iron glazes

Transparent glazes – hitting the eutectic

The eutectic is the mixture with the minimum melting or freezing point. The eutectic point is the temperature at which this eutectic melts or freezes.

Transparent glazes are 'perfect' glazes in the sense that the fluxes, the alumina and the silica will be in just the right proportions for them to melt together and form a clear glass. All of the oxides will enter the glass structure and become dissolved within it, and the colourless liquid that is formed will give a bright, shiny and transparent surface. From a practical point of view, this will also be the strongest and best-fitting combination of these materials that you can find.

Finding a transparent glaze

The set of glaze tests 1–49 have been designed to search across the main field in which glazes occur. They use some typical stoneware glaze ingredients: nepheline syenite, dolomite, whiting, china clay and quartz, and the position for each of these 49 glazes is plotted on the accompanying graph (see Fig. 7). The idea behind the experiment is to see if we can find the ratio of alumina:silica that gives the best transparent glaze.

The photograph on p.25 shows a 1.5 cm x 1.5 cm (0.6 in. x 0.6 in.) area for each of these tests fired on a buff clay body to cone 9. The two 'best' transparent glazes, nos. 19 and 26, are identi-

fied with a large red dot. However, the tests nos. 12, 18, 20, 25, 27 and 32 are also transparent glazes or virtually so, just not quite as bright as 19 and 26; they are each identified with a smaller red dot. We can see that there is actually only one transparent area and that it is found between 10–17.5% alumina and 60–70% silica. Fortunately for stoneware potters this 'best' transparent area is consistent for glazes made from all the usual glaze ingredients, i.e. any feldspar, any clay, and the fluxes containing the alkaline earths; calcium oxide (CaO) and magnesium oxide (MgO). The size of this transparent area will expand with increasing temperature/heat-work.

Transparent glaze No.1 (called TRA 1) is based on this set of tests. It falls between 19 and 26 and is in the middle of this best melted area. We can see from the photograph of the fired tests (see

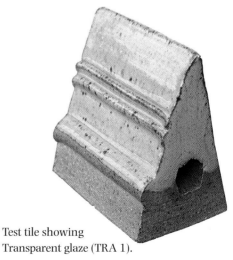

Test tile showing
Transparent glaze (TRA 1).

49 recipes followed by their simplified % analysis of alumina:silica

Recipes	1	2	3	4	5	6	7
Nepheline syenite	34.1	29.3	24.4	19.6	14.7	9.9	5.0
China clay	20.8	24.6	28.4	32.2	36.0	39.8	43.6
Dolomite	34.5	29.7	24.9	20.1	15.2	10.4	5.6
Whiting	5.3	4.6	3.8	3.1	2.3	1.6	0.8
Quartz	5.3	11.9	18.5	25.2	31.8	38.4	45.0
Al_2O_3	20.0	20.0	20.0	20.0	20.0	20.0	20.0
SiO_2	45.0	50.0	55.0	60.0	65.0	70.0	75.0

Recipes	8	9	10	11	12	13	14
Nepheline syenite	31.0	27.1	23.1	19.2	15.3	11.3	7.4
China clay	17.3	20.5	23.7	26.8	30.0	33.2	36.3
Dolomite	36.4	31.7	27.1	22.4	17.7	13.1	8.4
Whiting	6.9	5.9	5.0	4.1	3.1	2.2	1.3
Quartz	8.4	14.8	21.1	27.5	33.9	40.2	46.6
Al_2O_3	17.5	17.5	17.5	17.5	17.5	17.5	17.5
SiO_2	45.0	50.0	55.0	60.0	65.0	70.0	75.0

Recipes	15	16	17	18	19	20	21
Nepheline syenite	27.9	24.9	21.9	18.9	15.8	12.8	9.8
China clay	13.9	16.4	18.9	21.5	24.0	26.5	29.1
Dolomite	38.3	33.8	29.3	24.8	20.2	15.7	11.2
Whiting	8.4	7.3	6.2	5.1	4.0	2.9	1.8
Quartz	11.5	17.6	23.7	29.9	36.0	42.1	48.2
Al_2O_3	15.0	15.0	15.0	15.0	15.0	15.0	15.0
SiO_2	45.0	50.0	55.0	60.0	65.0	70.0	75.0

Recipes	22	23	24	25	26	27	28
Nepheline syenite	24.8	22.7	20.6	18.5	16.4	14.3	12.2
China clay	10.4	12.3	14.2	16.1	18.0	19.9	21.8
Dolomite	40.3	35.9	31.5	27.1	22.7	18.3	14.0
Whiting	10.0	8.7	7.4	6.1	4.8	3.5	2.3
Quartz	14.6	20.5	26.3	32.2	38.1	43.9	49.8
Al_2O_3	12.5	12.5	12.5	12.5	12.5	12.5	12.5
SiO_2	45.0	50.0	55.0	60.0	65.0	70.0	75.0

Recipes	29	30	31	32	33	34	35
Nepheline syenite	21.7	20.5	19.3	18.2	17.0	15.8	14.6
China clay	6.9	8.2	9.5	10.7	12.0	13.3	14.5
Dolomite	42.2	37.9	33.7	29.5	25.2	21.0	16.7
Whiting	11.5	10.0	8.6	7.1	5.7	4.2	2.7
Quartz	17.7	13.3	28.9	34.6	40.2	45.8	51.4
Al_2O_3	10.0	10.0	10.0	10.0	10.0	10.0	10.0
SiO_2	45.0	50.0	55.0	60.0	65.0	70.0	75.0

Recipes	36	37	38	39	40	41	42
Nepheline syenite	18.6	18.3	18.1	17.8	17.5	17.3	17.0
China clay	3.5	4.1	4.7	5.4	6.0	6.6	7.3
Dolomite	44.1	40.0	35.9	31.8	27.7	23.6	19.5
Whiting	13.1	11.4	9.8	8.1	6.5	4.9	3.2
Quartz	20.8	26.2	31.5	36.9	42.3	47.6	53.0
Al_2O_3	7.5	7.5	7.5	7.5	7.5	7.5	7.5
SiO_2	45.0	50.0	55.0	60.0	65.0	70.0	75.0

Recipes	43	44	45	46	47	48	49
Nepheline syenite	15.5	16.2	16.8	17.5	18.1	18.8	19.4
China clay	0.0	0.0	0.0	0.0	0.0	0.0	0.0
Dolomite	46.0	42.1	38.1	34.2	30.2	26.3	22.3
Whiting	14.6	12.8	11.0	9.2	7.3	5.5	3.7
Quartz	23.9	29.0	34.1	39.3	44.4	49.5	54.6
Al_2O_3	5.0	5.0	5.0	5.0	5.0	5.0	5.0
SiO_2	45.0	50.0	55.0	60.0	65.0	70.0	75.0

Fig.6, p.25) that at cone 9 there is a certain degree of latitude, and that we do not have to hit an exact spot to find an acceptable transparent glaze. We could, in fact, vary the amounts in this recipe for all of the ingredients by 1 or 2% and still keep within the transparent area.

TRA 1. Transparent glaze, cone 8–10.

Nepheline syenite	16.0
China clay	21.0
Dolomite	22.0
Whiting	6.0
Quartz	35.0
	100.0

% analysis of base glaze:
SiO_2 64.76; Al_2O_3 14.25; FeO 0.03; CaO 12.33; MgO 5.72; K_2O 0.95; Na_2O 1.95

Some other considerations

Although finding the best alumina:silica ratio for making a transparent glaze is very informative, it is only part of the story.

The slop glaze

The eutectic for Cornish stone and whiting is the very simple glaze TRA 2 (see below).

TRA 2. Transparent glaze, cone 9–11.

Cornish stone	85.0
Whiting	15.0
	100.0

% analysis of base glaze:
SiO_2 67.39; TiO_2 0.06; P_2O_5 0.43; Al_2O_3 14.12; FeO 0.11; CaO 10.49; MgO 0.12; K_2O 4.11; Na_2O 3.17

However, this glaze has a few problems; the main one being the absence of any clay which will help the slop glaze (see Glossary) stay in suspension and give handling strength to the glaze whilst the pot is being packed in the kiln. A glaze such as the Leach 4,3,2,1 transparent (see p.27) overcomes these problems. Not only has clay been introduced into the recipe but it is also an easy recipe to remember – just in case you mislay your recipe book!

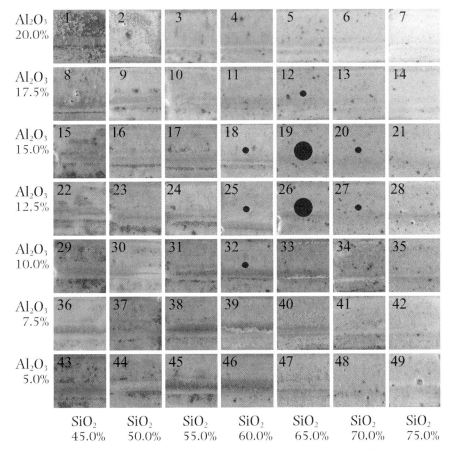

(Fig. 6) Photograph of tests 1–49. The two best transparent glazes are each indicated with a large red dot.

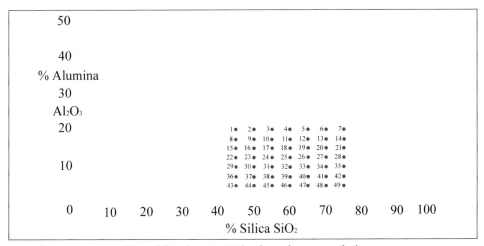

(Fig. 7) Plotting the position of the glazes 1–49 by their alumina and silica percentages.

The same glaze Transparent No.1 fired to cone 9 in reduction on four different clay bodies:

TOP LEFT On a high iron (terracotta) clay.

TOP RIGHT On a handbuilding white clay containing 30% Molochite grog. The crazing is quite severe and is one of the problems encountered when using additions of Molochite (a china clay grog) to make a coarse white clay body.

BOTTOM LEFT On a smooth white body. Some crazing is present.

BOTTOM RIGHT On a buff body based on ball clays and fireclay. The glaze is a good fit on this body. The brown specks come from the iron pyrites in the fireclay.

TRA 3. The 4, 3, 2, 1 Leach transparent glaze, cone 8–10 (from A Potter's Book, *by Bernard Leach).*

Potash or soda feldspar	40.0
China clay	10.0
Whiting	20.0
Flint	30.0
	100.0

% analysis of base glaze:
SiO_2 67.87; Al_2O_3 12.63; FeO 0.04; CaO 12.65; K_2O 5.52; Na_2O 1.29

Many glaze recipes will also include suspenders such as bentonite, calcium chloride and carboxymethylcellulose (C.M.C. for short, thankfully!).

The fired glaze

The appearance of transparent glazes is particularly dependent on the underlying clay body, both in terms of colour and glaze fit. The tiles opposite show the transparent no.1 glaze fired to cone 9 over four other clays. The right-hand side of each tile has been rubbed over with a black marker pen to help show signs of crazing. In all probability anyone else making up this glaze would get a different effect. After all, they would be using different glaze materials, clay body and firing cycle. Even formulating a glaze recipe to match a chemical analysis using a different computer glaze calculation program may give slightly divergent results.

It may be found that using carbonates, e.g. $CaCO_3$ (chalk, limestone or whiting) as a source of calcium oxide CaO, produces fine bubbles within the glaze. These come from the evolution of the carbon dioxide gas CO_2. Alternative ingredients such as talc (a magnesium silicate) and wollastonite (a calcium silicate) can be used to overcome this problem, as in TRA 4 and TRA 5.

Bottle by 'Made in Cley', TRA 5 on Limoges porcelain. Glaze recipe attributed to Nigel Wood. *Photograph by Nigel Kelham.*

TRA 4. Transparent glaze. Cone 9–10 (from the author).

Cornish Stone	55.0
China clay	10.0
Bentonite	2.0
Talc	8.0
Wollastonite	21.0
Flint	4.0
	100.0

% analysis of base glaze:
SiO_2 67.59; TiO_2 0.04; P_2O_5 0.27; Al_2O_3 13.14; FeO 0.24; CaO 11.36; MgO 2.77; K_2O 2.62; Na_2O 1.97

Cups and saucers by Joanna Howells, TRA 9 transparent glaze on 'Southern Ice' porcelain.

TRA 5. *Transparent 'porcelain white' glaze, cone 10–11 (from Nigel Wood).*

Potash feldspar	25.0
China clay	12.5
Hyplas 71 (a high silica ball clay)	12.5
Talc	3.0
Wollastonite	27.0
Flint	20.0
	100.0

% analysis of base glaze:
SiO_2 68.37; TiO_2 0.23; Al_2O_3 12.28; FeO 0.24; CaO 13.27; MgO 1.02; K_2O 3.60; Na_2O 1.00

Transparent glazes, using boric oxide

The preceding transparent glazes have been fired towards the top-end of the stoneware range. Boric oxide is a very useful addition if the potter wishes to bring the firing down to below cone 9 or improve glaze fit. Here are just a few examples:

TRA 6. *Transparent glaze, cone 6–8.*

Potash or soda feldspar	33.6
Standard borax frit	14.5
China clay	11.8
Bentonite	2.0
Dolomite	4.4
Whiting	11.0
Flint	22.7
	100.0

% analysis of base glaze:
SiO_2 64.00; Al_2O_3 13.5; B_2O_3 3.00; FeO 0.14; CaO 10.89; MgO 1.14; K_2O 4.86; Na_2O 2.47

TRA 7. *Transparent glaze, cone 8.*

Potash feldspar	31.6
Standard borax frit	6.3
China clay	9.4
Bentonite	2.0
Dolomite	12.5
Whiting	12.5
Flint	25.7
	100.0

Wood-fired, raw glazed dish using TRA 10, by Christine McCole and Roger Brann.

% analysis of base glaze:
SiO$_2$ 63.00; Al$_2$O$_3$ 12.00; B$_2$O$_3$ 1.36; FeO 0.17; CaO 13.88; MgO 3.20; K$_2$O 4.69; Na$_2$O 1.70

TRA 8. *Marcia Selsor's clear glaze, cone 6.*

Nepheline syenite	26.1
Gerstley borate	4.7
EPK China clay	19.0
Whiting	18.7
Flint	31.5
	100.0

% analysis of base glaze:
SiO$_2$ 65.0; P$_2$O$_5$ 0.06; Al$_2$O$_3$ 15.5; B$_2$O$_3$ 1.48; FeO 0.17; CaO 13.20; MgO 0.05; K$_2$O 1.45; Na$_2$O 3.09

Better melting (greater transparency) can also be achieved by using finer glaze ingredients to increase the contact between the particles. The potter could buy more finely-ground materials and push the slop glaze through a 200s mesh sieve or use a ball mill. For example, the following glaze is actually just outside the transparent area shown on the graph Fig. 8 and yet ball-milling for two hours had two effects: it improved the suspension of the slop glaze, and semi-opaque patches in the fired glaze disappeared.

TRA 9. *Clear, well-fitting bluish transparent porcelain glaze, cone 10 (from Joanna Howells).*

Cornish stone	54.5
China clay	10.2
Bentonite	1.7
Dolomite	4.6
Wollastonite	15.2
Flint	13.8
	100.0

% analysis of base glaze:
SiO$_2$ 70.37; TiO$_2$ 0.04; P$_2$O$_5$ 0.27; Al$_2$O$_3$ 13.26; FeO 0.17; CaO 10.10; MgO 1.18; K$_2$O 2.63; Na$_2$O 1.98

Transparent raw glazes

Traditional once-fired glazes have a fairly high clay content, typically 30–40%, which enables them to shrink in step with the clay body as it dries. Ball clays that are low in alumina and high in silica-high clay can be very useful in this situation as they don't unbalance the glaze with too much Al_2O_3.

TRA 10. Transparent raw glaze, cone 10 (from Christine McCole and Roger Brann).

Potash feldspar	30.0
Ball clay (HV)	30.0
Dolomite	20.0
Flint	20.0
	100.0

% analysis of base glaze:
SiO_2 66.08; TiO_2 0.53; Al_2O_3 14.92; FeO 0.32; CaO 7.23; MgO 4.93; K_2O 4.92; Na_2O 1.07

Potter's notes: The glaze used on the inside of this dish is applied quite thickly to leatherhard pots by dipping and pouring ('double cream' thickness). In this example, TRA10 has been coloured to make a semi-opaque, buff glaze by adding 5.0% zirconium silicate and 3.0% manganese dioxide. It covers well and is not used over incised decoration for this reason.

In a reduction firing many transparent glazes pick up a green or bluish colour from iron oxide in the clay body or from traces in the glaze ingredients. This leads us neatly into the next section – Celadons.

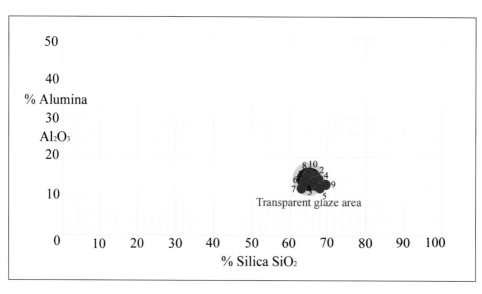

(Fig. 8) This graph shows, with concentric red circles, the transparent area that was found using the set of 1–49 tests discussed at the beginning of this chapter. The TRA 1–10 transparent glazes that are given as actual recipes are also plotted on the graph.

Dish by Joanna Howells using CEL 1, a pale turquoise crackle glaze over porcelain.

Celadons

Celadons range in colour from light blue to dark olive, including blue-greens, grey-greens and yellow-greens, and are produced by iron in a reduced state entering solution in a clear or semi-transparent glaze. The iron may be introduced in various forms. The most usual is to add between 0.5% and 3% Fe_2O_3 (ferric oxide) as straight red iron oxide, but it may also be brought into the glaze as an iron-bearing clay. Black iron oxide (ferrous FeO) or iron spangles (Fe_3O_4) can also be used, but may not disperse quite so well, giving a slightly blotchy appearance. Iron can also come into the glaze from the underlying clay body. Indeed, once you start reduction firing, it is very difficult to produce transparent glazes that aren't actually celadons! (see the transparent glaze T1 on p.24).

The celadon recipes in this chapter have been arranged to run approximately from the lightest to the darkest. Helpful comments and notes by the potters who supplied the recipes are included with each glaze.

CEL 1. Pale turquoise crackle glaze, cone 10 (from Joanna Howell).

Potash feldspar	32.0
China clay	16.0
Whiting	3.2
Wood ash	32.0
Flint	16.8
	100.0

% analysis of base glaze:
SiO_2 60.41; Al_2O_3 16.36; FeO 1.21; CaO 11.76; MgO 1.46; K_2O 5.04; Na_2O 2.51; other oxides 1.25

Potter's notes: This glaze was developed from a triaxial blend and uses a wood ash that is low in iron.

Vase by Joanna Howells using CEL 2 blue crackle celadon over porcelain.

CEL 2. Blue crackle celadon, cone 10 (from Joanna Howell).

Potash feldspar	78.9
Barium carbonate	2.0
Whiting	9.5
Flint	9.6
	100.0

Bentonite (as suspender)	2–3%
Red iron oxide	1.0

Plus calcium chloride to suspend the slop glaze.

% analysis of base glaze:
SiO_2 64.46; Al_2O_3 15.29; FeO 0.07; CaO 5.9; K_2O 10.25; Na_2O 2.4

Potter's notes: Because of the lack of clay in the recipe, it is helpful, although not essential, to ball-mill the glaze for 2 hours. The flocculant calcium chloride is then added to the slop glaze to thicken and help act as a suspender. This glaze needs a thick application and strong reduction in the firing to produce the blue colour; otherwise it tends towards a blue-grey.

CEL 3. Blue celadon, cone 9–10 (from Margaret Frith).

Cornish stone	22.0
China clay	10.0
Molochite	18.0
Whiting	23.0
Flint/quartz	27.0
	100.0

Red iron oxide	0.75

% analysis of base glaze:
SiO_2 65.11; TiO_2 0.03; P_2O_5 0.11; Al_2O_3 16.95; FeO 0.25; CaO 14.77; MgO 0.14; K_2O 1.77; Na_2O 0.87

Potter's notes: The glaze is improved by milling for 2 to 3 hours.

Porcelain round lidded box by Margaret Frith using CEL 3 blue celadon glaze.

Blue-green celadon bowl using CEL 4 by John Britt.

CEL 4. *Blue-green celadon, cone 9–10 (from John Britt).*

Potash feldspar	24.0
Grolleg china clay	19.0
Barnard slip *	2.8
Barium carbonate	1.9
Whiting	19.0
Flint	33.3
	100.0
Tin oxide	1.0

[* Or any other high-iron clay]

% analysis of base glaze:
SiO_2 67.37; TiO_2 0.03; Al_2O_3 13.87; FeO 0.60; BaO 1.68; CaO 12.20; K_2O 3.47; Na_2O 0.78

Potter's notes: To get a blue-green, rather than a grey-green glaze, it is essential to use a low titanium kaolin such as 'Grolleg' in both the glaze and the body. The body recipe for these pots is Grolleg kaolin 55; silica 25; custer feldspar 25; bentonite 3.

CEL 5. *Celadon glaze, cone 6–7 (from Marcia Selsor).*

Nepheline syenite	26.1
Gerstley borate frit	4.7
EPK China clay	19.0
Whiting	18.7
Flint	31.5
	100.0
Red iron oxide	1.5

% analysis of base glaze:
SiO_2 65.07; P_2O_5 0.06; Al_2O_3 15.42; B_2O_3 1.47; FeO 0.18; CaO 13.00; MgO 0.02; K_2O 1.56; Na_2O 3.22

Potter's notes: This is a transparent base glaze with an addition of 1.5% red iron oxide. The firings are quite fast: 7–8 hours in either a $1.1m^3$ (40 cu. ft) or $1.6 m^3$ (60 cu. ft) kiln. Reduction starts at cone 09, then light to neutral up to cone 6 with 45 minutes soak at heavier reduction.

CEL 6. *Celadon glaze, cone 9–10*
(from the author).

Cornish stone	65.4
China clay	7.7
Whiting	11.5
Flint/quartz	15.4
	100.0
Red iron oxide	2.0

% analysis of base glaze:
SiO_2 71.50; TiO_2 0.05; P_2O_5 0.35;
Al_2O_3 14.50; FeO 0.10; CaO 8.29;
K_2O 2.60; Na_2O 2.61

Potter's notes: This glaze was 'discovered' whilst doing a progression test to try and sort out why a tenmoku glaze was coming out too brown. The test started by adding 2% red iron oxide into the base glaze (giving this glaze) and then going up in 2% additions of red iron oxide.

Top: Detail of vase with a modelled dragon, using CEL 5, by Marcia Selsor.

Right: Butter dish by the author with red iron oxide brushwork decoration, and CEL 6.

A lidded box by John Harlow using CEL 7.

CEL 7. Celadon glaze, cone 9–10 (from John Harlow).

FFF Potash feldspar	45.0
Standard borax frit	5.0
China clay	10.0
Local yellow clay	5.0
Barium carbonate	5.0
Whiting	10.0
Flint	20.0
	100.0

% analysis of base glaze:

SiO_2 64.82; TiO_2 0.06; P_2O_5 0.06; Al_2O_3 15.42; B_2O_3 1.02; FeO 0.15; BaO 4.19; CaO 7.32; MgO 0.02; K_2O 3.90; Na_2O 3.04

Potter's notes: The yellow clay in this recipe is dug from my paddock. The clay on its own fires to a beautiful orange at around 980°C (1796°F) and contains sufficient iron to produce the soft green-blue of a typical celadon, but one could use almost any ball clay with the addition of small amounts (1–2%) of iron oxide.

CEL 8. Celadon glaze, cone 10–11 (from David Winkley).

FFF feldspar	43.1
High temp. borax frit	0.4
Calcined china clay	2.8
Ball clay (high silica)	10.7
Bentonite	0.8
Barium carbonate	2.7
Dolomite	11.1
Flint	28.4
	100.0
Red iron oxide	2.5

% analysis of base glaze:

SiO_2 71.6; TiO_2 0.19; P_2O_5 0.06; Al_2O_3 12.47; B_2O_3 0.07; FeO 0.18; CaO 4.27; MgO 2.67; K_2O 3.74; Na_2O 2.49

Potter's notes: This is a good-fitting base glaze which can be used either on its own or under an iron glaze. Its high silica content helps to heighten iron brushwork which flashes red. The glaze is ball-milled

Wax-resist decorated jug by David Winkley showing CEL 8 underneath a kaki glaze.

for three hours. It has a tendency to gather at rims and inside edges of bowls unless carefully dipped, although any unevenness seems to disappear provided it has a long, hot firing. Using less red iron oxide, e.g. 0.5–1% gives a paler celadon and a blue version can be made by substituting 2% cobalt carbonate for the iron (shown on p.91).

A lidded serving dish by 'Made in Cley' using CEL 9. *Photograph by Richard Kelham.*

CEL 9. Dark celadon glaze, cone 10–11
(from 'Made in Cley').

Potash feldspar	70.0
China clay	10.0
Whiting	10.0
Flint/quartz	10.0
	100.0
Red iron oxide	3.0

% analysis of base glaze:
SiO_2 64.41; Al_2O_3 17.93; FeO 0.06; CaO 6.24; K_2O 9.21; Na_2O 2.15

Potter's notes: Needs to be thickly applied, fired to cone 10, with strong reduction. The glaze pools nicely and is good over incised decoration. We also do brushwork decoration, using red iron oxide, on top of the dry glaze.

CEL 10. Celadon glaze, cone 11
(from 'Made in Cley').

Potash feldspar	60.0
China clay	5.0
Whiting	10.0
Flint/quartz	25.0
	100.0
Red iron oxide	3.0

% analysis of base glaze:
SiO_2 70.36; Al_2O_3 13.77; FeO 0.05; CaO 6.15; K_2O 7.83; Na_2O 1.83

Potter's notes: With only 3% red iron oxide, this glaze is a serviceable celadon but needs to be applied fairly thickly, although not too thickly as it can craze. A slow cool also assists glaze fit. A 7% addition of red iron oxide to this base produces the tenmoku TEN 8 on p.78.

CEL 11. *Celadon glaze, cone 9–10 (from Melanie Brown).*

Potash feldspar	50.0
Standard borax frit	5.0
China clay	10.0
Dolomite	5.0
Whiting	5.0
Flint/quartz	25.0
	100.0

Red iron oxide	2.0

% analysis of base glaze:
SiO_2 69.02; Al_2O_3 14.42; B_2O_3 1.00; FeO 0.04; CaO 5.69; MgO 1.17; K_2O 6.66; Na_2O 2.01

Potter's notes: This is a stable glaze with quite a wide firing range. I ball-mill the iron to prevent too much speckle. Works equally well on porcelain or stoneware.

CEL 12. *Dark amber celadon glaze, cone 9–10 (from John Britt).*

Alberta slip	35.9
Potash (custer) feldspar	21.7
Gerstley borate	3.3
China clay	3.3
Whiting	7.6
Wollastonite	14.1
Flint/quartz	14.1
	100.0

Yellow ochre	8.7

% analysis of base glaze:
SiO_2 64.59; TiO_2 0.16; Al_2O_3 11.47; B_2O_3 0.98; FeO 1.88; CaO 14.99; MgO 1.05; K_2O 3.72; Na_2O 1.16

Potter's notes: I soak at the top of the firing in oxidation when cone 9 is half over and cone 10 is just starting to bend.

CEL 10 with red iron oxide decoration on a bottle by 'Made in Cley'.

Teapot and lidded pot by Melanie Brown using CEL 11.

CEL 12 on a lidded dish with incised decoration by John Britt.

After ten minutes or so when cone 10 is at '3 o'clock' I turn off and allow a natural cool. The kiln is opened 18–24 hours later. I like to open it cold. The illustrations show the glaze from firing in two different kilns.

CEL 13. Dark green transparent raw glaze, cone 9–10 (from Christine McCole and Roger Brann).

Potash feldspar	9.8
Red clay powder	45.0
Magnesium carbonate	1.1
Whiting	26.0
Flint/quartz	18.1
	100.0

% analysis of base glaze:
SiO_2 61.16; TiO_2 0.43; Al_2O_3 12.22; FeO 4.45; CaO 18.03; MgO 0.74; K_2O 1.94; Na_2O 0.99

Potter's notes: Originally an Andrew Holden recipe. We use Potclays 1135/2 red S.E. for the powdered red clay. The glaze is applied thickly on leatherhard pots. It can drip and run quite a lot so use with care. Very tough for single firing, with excellent resistance to flaking when on raw pots.

CEL 12 glazed Buddha by John Britt.

Once-fired jug by Christine McCole and Roger Brann using CEL 13.

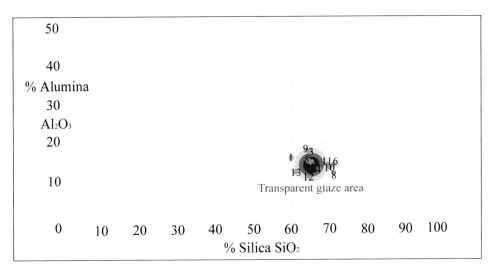

(Fig. 9) The $Al_2O_3:SiO_2$ positions for CEL 1–CEL 13 in relation to the 'transparent glaze area'.

The $Al_2O_3:SiO_2$ positions for CEL 1 to CEL 13 are shown on the graph above and indicate the close relationship between celadons and glazes that are in, or close to, the transparent area.

This chapter has interpreted celadon fairly loosely, as any transparent or semi-transparent blue-green-grey glaze created through the addition of a small percentage of reduced iron. The classic celadons are viscous, feldspathic, semi-transparent glazes and are produced by:
- The $Al_2O_3:SiO_2$ position being at the high silica side of the transparent area
- A thick glaze application
- The presence of minute air bubbles
- Microcrystallization due to slow cooling

The colour is enhanced by:
- Thick application over a light body
- Low amounts of titanium oxide and iron for blues
- High levels of titanium oxide for yellows
- The darker celadons, often called 'northern celadons', need around 4% red iron oxide – this may just be present in the glaze or result as a combination of iron in the glaze and the clay body

As several potters have noted, the bases for celadons can also be used as the starting point for making the dark brown glazes called 'tenmokus'.

The next three sections investigate unbalancing the eutectic glaze composition by increasing:

1. The alkalis (fluxes)
2. The alumina
3. The silica

The high alkaline glazes

Ash glazes

Wood ash can make an excellent ingredient for producing a variety of beautiful, shiny satin or matt glazes, often with just a few other materials. Indeed, wood ash can be used on its own. A thin waft or wash of wood ash usually produces an orange blush on the surface of the work, and the deliberate raking of the firebox in wood-fired kilns can be used to encourage fly-ash to settle on the ware. The ash then reacts with the alumina and silica in the clay body to form a glaze.

The reason that one can use these satisfyingly simple recipes is that wood ashes, and indeed many other local materials, are quite complex. Thus by using just one ingredient called 'wood ash' we are in fact putting in a whole host of chemicals and trace elements. These are drawn up from the earth and utilised by the plant to form complex carbon-based organic molecules. In burning the plant we 'liberate' most of the carbon, nitrogen and oxygen back into the atmosphere. In fact, for trees and shrubs, over 99% of their weight is lost in this way; leaving a very small residue of glaze-forming inorganic molecules.

The analyses for a few wood ashes are

Pot by Malcolm Jepson glazed in situ with fly-ash.

Vase by Mike Dodd using his 'standard' ash, ASH 1.

given in the appendix (see p.122). However, they shouldn't be given too much credence as the data can vary quite widely according to differing sources of information. It is not that any are necessarily wrong, but that ash analyses can differ depending on:

- The part of the plant that is burnt – branches are different to main limbs
- The season
- Collecting conditions, including contamination
- How much it is washed – each change of water removes soluble fluxes
- Temperature of firing

For these reasons, the base glaze analyses in this section are presented as approximations.

Ashes typically fall into two categories. Trees and shrubs are high in the fluxes potassium and calcium and very low in silica and alumina. An important constituent can be phosphorous pentoxide (P_2O_5) which helps produce the Jun effect seen with some ash glaze recipes. The grasses, on the other hand, are very high in silica and consequently low in everything else. An average composition for trees and grasses, and an indication of the rather broad range of values for the oxides, are given in the table below.

Table A. Average fired analysis for trees and shrubs

	%	range
SiO_2	12	1 – 40
P_2O_5	5	1 – 14
Al_2O_3	6	1 – 16
Fe_2O_3	1	1 – 3
CaO	52	20 – 80
MgO	5	4 – 12
MnO	1	0 – 4
K_2O	10	5 – 20
Na_2O	5	1 – 10
Other	3	1 – 3

Table B. Average fired analysis for grasses.

	%	range
SiO_2	65	50 – 90
P_2O_5	5	2 – 10
Al_2O_3	5	1 – 16
Fe_2O_3	1	1 – 3
CaO	8	4 – 20
MgO	3	4 – 10
MnO	–	0 – 1
K_2O	8	5 – 20
Na_2O	3	1 – 6
Other	2	1 – 3

Synthetic wood ashes

Collecting and preparing wood ash by washing and sieving or even ball-milling can be an arduous task. It is a material that needs to be handled with care because of its caustic, highly alkaline nature. Also, because each batch of ash is different, it can be time-consuming to test it and there is no guarantee that a worthwhile glaze will be found. It is not surprising, therefore, that potters have come up with recipes that seek to emulate wood ash by using more consistent glaze ingredients. The following synthetic wood ash emulates their high flux, low alumina and low silica composition. It can be substituted in recipes if no actual wood ash is available. The iron and manganese can be omitted for light-toned glazes or added to give greenish-brown colours.

Synthetic wood ash (for use in replacement of real wood ash).

Potash feldspar	5.0
Soda ash	5.0
High alkaline frit	17.0
Bone ash	8.0
Dolomite	15.0
Whiting	50.0
	100.0

Black or red iron oxide	0–4%
Manganese dioxide	0–4%

% analysis of this synthetic wood ash:
SiO_2 16.60; P_2O_5 5.13; Al_2O_3 2.66; B_2O_3 0.93; CaO 53.28; MgO 4.60; K_2O 4.99; Na_2O 11.81

The glazes that follow in this section are included as much for inspiration as in any real hope that one will be able to replicate them exactly – such is the nature and excitement of ash glazes!

Double-handled vase by Mike Dodd using the willow ash recipe ASH 2.

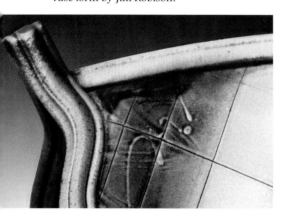

Above: ASH 3. Olive dish by Douglas Phillips.
Below: Dry ash glaze (ASH 4), detail of rim,
vase form by Jim Robison.

ASH 1. *Standard wood ash glaze, cone 10
(from Mike Dodd).*

FFF potash feldspar	40.0
Wood ash	40.0
Ball clay HP71	10.0
Local red clay	10.0
	100.0

*Approximate % analysis of base glaze
based on a generic analysis for wood ash:*
SiO_2 56; P_2O_5 2; Al_2O_3 16; FeO 2;
CaO 13; MgO 2; K_2O 5; Na_2O 4

ASH 2. *Willow ash glaze, cone 9–10
(from Mike Dodd).*

FFF potash feldspar	40.0
Willow ash	40.0
Ball clay HV	20.0
	100.0

Approximate % analysis of base glaze:
SiO_2 46; P_2O_5 2; Al_2O_3 13; FeO 2;
CaO 15; MgO 2; K_2O 14; Na_2O 6

ASH 3. *Douglas Phillips' green ash glaze,
cone 10.*

Local clay	70.0
Wood ash	30.0
	100.0

Approximate % analysis of base glaze:
SiO_2 49; P_2O_5 4; Al_2O_3 12; FeO 2;
CaO 12; MgO 3; K_2O 11; Na_2O 5;
other 2

Potter's notes: The local Queen Camel
clay is a sandy clay and is ball-milled for
20 minutes. The wood ash is elm. The
glaze is a yellowish to green Jun where
thicker and was developed for our summer
school courses as a raw glaze. It also
works well in the proportion local clay
60%, wood ash 40%.

ASH 4. *Dry ash glaze. Cone 8–9 (from Jim
Robison).*

Potash feldspar	10.4
Wood ash	41.6
China clay	37.6
Whiting	10.4
	100.0

% analysis of base glaze:
SiO_2 46; P_2O_5 1; Al_2O_3 22; FeO 2;
CaO 20; MgO 2; K_2O 4; Na_2O 3

Potter's notes: Most pieces are glazed
raw and once fired to cone 8 well over.
The firing is slowed down from 600°C–
800°C (1112°F–1472°F) for body carbon
burn out. Reduction starts at 1080°C
(1976°F) and is heavy for the first hour,
then light reduction with a final clean
burn for a few minutes before turning off.

ASH 6 on a squared-off bottle (height: 28 cm/11 in.) by Phil Rogers.

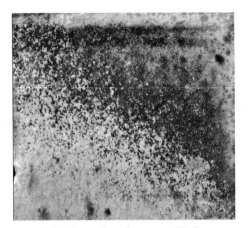

Test tile by the author showing ASH 5.

ASH 5. Dry ash glaze, cone 9–11 (from the author).

Wood ash	50.0
China clay	50.0
	100.0

% analysis of base glaze:
SiO_2 33; P_2O_5 2; Al_2O_3 22; FeO 1;
CaO 29; MgO 3; K_2O 7; Na_2O 3

Potter's notes: A well-known recipe.
Other clays at 50% will also produce
matt glazes and typically develop mottled
yellow and red colours.

ASH 6. Ash glaze, cone 11 (from Phil Rogers).

Potash feldspar	15.0
Kington stone	14.3
Cornish stone	8.5
China clay	2.6
Ball clay Hyplas 71	10.6
Whiting	8.5
Wood ash (mixed hardwood)	33.5
Bone ash	3.0
Flint	4.0
	100.0
Red iron oxide	

% analysis of base glaze:
SiO_2 52; P_2O_5 2; Al_2O_3 12; FeO 1;
CaO 22; MgO 2; K_2O 5; Na_2O 3; other 1

Potter's notes: This is a toffee-coloured
glaze similar to that which the Japanese
would call AME. It reacts well to certain
slips – for example, ball clay BLU 85%
and nepheline syenite 15%. (BLU used to
be called TWVD and is a ball clay containing 53% SiO2 and 32% Al_2O_3.) I like
ash glazes that run and change colour
and texture in the depressions made by
impressing or incising decoration. This
glaze is particularly good in that respect;
changing to a dark, almost black colour
in contrast to the pale background.

ASH 7. Kington stone and ash glaze, cone 11 (from Phil Rogers).

Potash feldspar	13.4
Kington stone	17.2
Cornish stone	13.8
Wood ash	33.4
Hyplas 71 (a high silica ball clay)	12.8
Whiting	7.4
Flint	2.0
	100.0
Red iron oxide	2.0

Approximate % analysis of base glaze:
SiO_2 56; Al_2O_3 12; FeO 1; CaO 19;
MgO 2; K_2O 5; Na_2O 3; other 2

Potter's notes: Kington stone contains
approximately 6% iron and I add a small
amount to achieve a good colour. A very
reliable glaze that seldom lets me down.
Thickness is important – too thin and
the result is an awful 'shoe polish'.

ASH 8. Phil Rogers' pine ash glaze, cone 11.

Potash feldspar	14.5
Cornish stone	14.5
Pine ash	53.0
China clay	6.0
Whiting	5.0
Quartz	7.0
	100.0

ASH 7 on a large thrown bottle (height: 45 cm/18 in.) with impressed pattern by Phil Rogers.
Photograph courtesy of the Pucker Gallery, Boston.

A tall bottle, (height: 58 cm/23 in.) using ASH 8 pine ash glaze, by Phil Rogers.

Bowl with 'Jumping Iron' decoration and ASH 9 by Brian Simmons.

Approximate % analysis of base glaze:
SiO_2 44; P_2O_5 2; Al_2O_3 13; FeO 2;
CaO 25; MgO 2; K_2O 8; Na_2O 3; other 1

Potter's notes: Far back in the mists of
time this glaze began life as the Leach
glaze: feldspar 40, ash 40, clay 20. It
was changed to reduce the maturing
temperature, which basically meant
increasing the ash and lowering the clay.
This is my most used and reliable glaze –
it has remained more or less unaltered
for 20 years. I like the variegated surface
that moves from shiny to crystalline
matt. This is best achieved by using a
white slip under the glaze. The present
recipe for this is 25% 200s-mesh
Molochite and 75% of a high silica,
low iron ball clay called Hyplas 71.

ASH 9. *Wood ash glaze, cone 9–10
(from Brian Simmons).*

Potash feldspar	40.0
Ball clay HV	13.0
Red clay	7.0
Wood ash	40.0
	100.0

Approximate % analysis of base glaze:
SiO_2 51; P_2O_5 2; Al_2O_3 15; FeO 1;
CaO 18; MgO 2; K_2O 8; Na_2O 3

Potter's notes: The red clay is Potclays
P1135/2, a high iron (9% Fe_2O_3) terracotta. The wood ash is mainly elm.

The Al_2O_3:SiO_2 positions for the ash glazes
in this chapter are plotted on the graph,
Fig. 10 (see p.70). This is a good example
of how useful the plotting-out of glazes on

a graph can be. It helps us to understand what is happening in a visual, rather than a numerical, way. We can see immediately, that compared with transparent glazes, these satiny ash glazes have the right amount of alumina but are 'unbalanced' in that they are high in fluxes and low in silica. This means that all of the silica and alumina are 'used up' in the glass formation and that a proportion of the fluxes will not be able to enter the melt. The fluxes, however, are in two distinct groups: alkalis and alkaline earths.

The alkalis

Potassium and soda are powerful fluxes and in wood ash are varyingly present in their soluble carbonate form. These will give off their CO_2 and melt around 900°C (1652°F). They will be the first fluxes to combine with the alumina and silica to form a glass.

The alkaline earths

Calcium and magnesium have a much higher eutectic melting point than the alkalis. The effect is that because the alkalis – potassium and soda – have been the first to 'grab' the alumina and silica, it will be the alkaline earths – calcium and magnesia – that are left out of the melt. This preferential bonding can be seen in the close-up (see above).

The shiny greenish-grey and heavily crazed area is the glass formation in which all the alkalis and silica are involved. The light greyish-buff matt areas come about through two processes: suspension and crystal formation. In glazes furthest away from the transparent areas – that is those glazes that are heavily overloaded with the alkaline earths – the calcium and magnesia will not enter the glass structure and will just stay suspended in the liquid, in

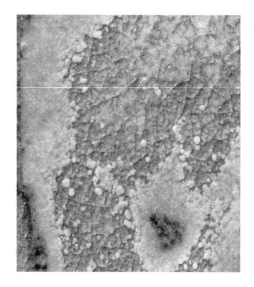

Test tile showing calcium and magnesium silicate crystals within a high alkaline, crazed glassy area.

just the same way as earth or fine sand can be stirred in water to discolour it. However, for glazes closer to the eutectic transparent area, the calcium and magnesia may have been dissolved in the glass, but have crystallised out of the solution as the glaze cools down. An analogy is the way table salt can be dissolved in boiling water to form a saturated solution but will drop out and form crystals as the liquid cools down.

The high alkaline and high alumina glazes

The similarity between wood ash glazes and 'ordinary' glazes that are unbalanced by excessive fluxes can be seen in the photograph in Fig. 6 (see p.25). The glazes with less than 60% silica, (i.e. to the left of the transparent area) could all pass as versions of wood ash glazes! The next three glazes, apart from being highly alkaline, also contain increasingly high levels of alumina.

HAA 1. Satin, crackle, semi-transparent, cone 9–10 (from Glyn and Victor Harris).

Potash feldspar	45.0
China clay	12.0
Bentonite	1.0
Barium carbonate	5.0
Dolomite	9.0
Whiting	17.0
Flint/quartz	11.0
	100.0

Copper carbonate	0.5
Zirconium silicate	5.0
C.M.C.	4.0

% analysis of base glaze:
SiO_2 54.89; Al_2O_3 14.91; FeO 0.19; CaO 14.67; MgO 2.33; BaO 4.53; K_2O 6.86; Na_2O 1.62

HAA 2. Light oatmeal, satin matt glaze, cone 9–10 (from Glyn and Victor Harris).

Potash feldspar	48.0
China clay	10.0
Ball clay (AK)	10.0
(a high alumina ball clay)	
Dolomite	20.0
Whiting	7.0
Flint/quartz	5.0
	100.0

% analysis of base glaze:
SiO_2 54.54; TiO_2 0.14; Al_2O_3 18.64; FeO 0.25; CaO 12.15; MgO 5.10; K_2O 7.45; Na_2O 1.73

Potter's notes: HAA 1 and HAA 2 are mainly used as once-firing brush-on glazes. The glaze ingredients are mixed with water to a normal dipping thickness for bisque-fired pots. This gives the correct powder to water ratio and the C.M.C. is stirred in as a thickener.

HAA 3. Dolomite matt glaze, cone 9 (from John Harlow).

FFF potash feldspar	27.8
Nepheline syenite	10.2
China clay	25.8
Dolomite	8.5
Whiting	16.5
Mixed wood ash	6.1
Flint/quartz	5.1
	100.0
Yellow ochre	3.0

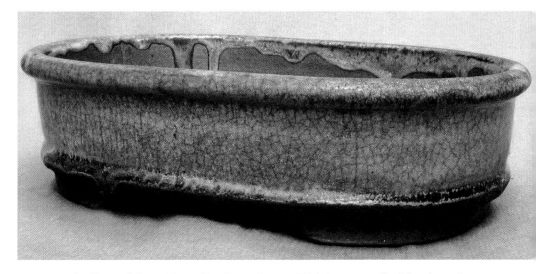

Bonsai tray by Glyn and Victor Harris (Erin Pottery), using HAA 1 as a once-fired, brush-on glaze. A thin copper wash has been applied to the foot-ring. The crazing lines have been stained with ink.

Rectangular bonsai dish by Glyn and Victor Harris, using HAA 2 as a once-fired, brush-on glaze. A thin copper wash has been applied to the foot-ring.

% analysis of base glaze:
SiO_2 52.22; P_2O_5 0.26; Al_2O_3 21.70; FeO 0.34; CaO 16.45; MgO 2.50; K_2O 3.26; Na_2O 3.27

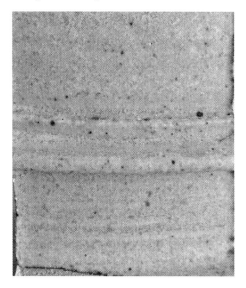

HAA 3. Test tile by John Harlow.

The high alumina glazes

Semi-transparent satin and satin matts

The area that plots-out above the transparent region on the Al_2O_3:SiO_2 graph (see Fig. 7, p.25) produces some beautiful satin and matt high alumina glazes. The glazes numbered 5, 13, 14, 20 and 21, given on p.23 and illustrated in Fig.6 (see p.25) are of this type. They tend to be rather subtle, quiet glazes with certain practical advantages. The high alumina content means that plenty of clay can be used in the recipe, to aid suspension as a slop glaze. The low flux content makes for stability so that the glaze, and any decoration using colouring metal oxides, shows little tendency to run during the firing. Here are five examples:

ALU 1. *Semi-transparent, satin glaze, cone 10–11 (from David Winkley).*

FFF potash feldspar	14.6
Petalite	9.1
Cornish stone	38.7
China clay	10.6
Ball clay TWVD	8.6
Bentonite	1.0
Magnesium carbonate	2.3
Dolomite	2.9
Whiting	8.2
Flint/quartz	4.0
	100.0

% analysis of base glaze:
SiO_2 65.03; TiO_2 0.14; P_2O_5 0.22; Al_2O_3 19.12; FeO 0.31; CaO 6.73; MgO 1.97; K_2O 3.52; Na_2O 2.48; Li_2O 0.48

ALU 2. *Alumina satin matt, cone 8–10.*

Potash feldspar	45.6
China clay	13.7
Ball clay (AK) (high in alumina)	9.0
Dolomite	9.0
Whiting	9.0
Flint/quartz	13.7
	100.0

% analysis of base glaze:
SiO_2 61.52; TiO_2 0.12; Al_2O_3 18.42; FeO 0.25; CaO 8.98; MgO 2.22; K_2O 6.88; Na_2O 1.61

Shown on the inside of the jug by Paul Stubbs on p.102.

ALU 3. *Satin glaze with very small crystals, cone 9–10 (from Joanna Howells).*

Potash feldspar	35.0
Calcium borate frit	5.0
China clay	21.0
Magnesium carbonate	7.0
Whiting	15.0
Flint/quartz	17.0
	100.0

% analysis of base glaze:
SiO_2 58.36; Al_2O_3 17.30; B_2O_3 2.92; FeO 0.03; CaO 11.40; MgO 3.82; K_2O 5.00; Na_2O 1.17

Bowl by David Winkley using ALU 1.

ALU 3 on a porcelain ('Southern Ice') bowl by Joanna Howells.

ALU 4. Satin, semi transparent, cone 9, (from Christine and Peter Penfold).

Nepheline syenite	17.0
China clay	34.0
Talc	12.0
Whiting	12.0
Flint/quartz	25.0
	100.0

% analysis of base glaze:
SiO_2 65.40; TiO_2 0.04; Al_2O_3 18.82; FeO 0.36; CaO 7.24; MgO 4.09; K_2O 1.57; Na_2O 2.48

Potter's notes: Ideal for the inside of functional pots such as casseroles. Dries hard on the bisque-fired pot; a glaze that is forgivingly easy to handle before firing and gives very consistent results.

ALU 5. Satin white, cone 9 (from John Harlow).

Potash feldspar	15.0
Nepheline syenite	5.0
Cornish stone	30.0
Standard borax frit	3.0
China clay	13.0
Ball clay Hymod AT	5.0
Barium carbonate	5.0
Whiting	7.0
Flint/quartz	17.0
	100.0

ALU 5 shown on a test tile by John Harlow.

Squared-off dish by Christine and Peter Penfold with ALU 4 as a liner glaze.

% analysis of base glaze:
SiO_2 66.65; TiO_2 0.09; P_2O_5 0.15; Al_2O_3 16.49; B_2O_3 0.61; FeO 0.17; CaO 5.26; MgO 0.07; BaO 4.17; K_2O 3.91; Na_2O 2.43

Shinos

Shinos are white, virtually opaque glazes tinged with orange – although this may range from a light orange-brown blush through to a deep burnt red. A characteristic of these glazes is that they are high in the powerful fluxing alkalis K_2O and Na_2O and low in the alkaline earths CaO and MgO. This is thought to favour the crystallisation of Fe_2O_3 rather than producing the blue, honey or green colours that come from the iron being in solution. The relatively high proportion of alkalis are held in check, so that the glaze is not too fluid, by the high amount of alumina. Nepheline syenite is frequently used in shino recipes as a source of these alkalis, and the iron (around 1–2%) may be introduced either from the body, an iron slip or as an iron-bearing clay in the glaze.

SHI 1. *White Shino, cone 9–10 (from Simone McDowell).*

Potash feldspar	34.0
Nepheline syenite	44.0
BBV ball clay (a high silica ball clay)	20.0
Potclay 1135 red (a terracotta clay)	2.0
	100.0

% analysis of base glaze:
SiO_2 64.85; TiO_2 0.02; Al_2O3 21.20; FeO 0.39; CaO 0.64; MgO 0.07; K_2O 6.84; Na_2O 5.68

Potter's notes: This dish shows the shino over a dark blue slip (made by adding 10% cobalt carbonate to a porcelain throwing body).

SHI 2. *Mark Melbourne's shino glaze, cone 11+.*

Soda feldspar	33.3
Nepheline syenite	33.3
Ball clay AT	33.3
	100.0

% analysis of base glaze:
SiO_2 63.23; TiO_2 0.42; Al_2O_3 24.56; FeO 0.77; CaO 0.69; MgO 0.14; K_2O 3.82; Na_2O 6.37

Potter's notes: The glaze is applied to leatherhard pots. These bowls were fired in a 3.4 m³ (120 cu. ft) wood kiln with an overall firing time of 50 hours. The colour varies, with brighter oranges when fired closed (e.g. bowls set rim to rim) and a darker, redder shino when fired open.

Press-moulded dish with resist decoration by Simone McDowell. SHI 1 over a dark blue slip.

Two bowls by Mark Melbourne using SHI 2.

Reduction begins at 900°C (1641°F), with a one hour clean fire to finish. Kiln is clammed up at 960°C (1760°F).

SHI 3. Meyer shino, cone 9–10 (from John Britt).

Nepheline syenite	47.7
China clay	28.0
Lithium carbonate	5.5
Whiting	2.3
Soda ash	5.5
Flint/quartz	11.0
	100.0
Tin oxide	9.0

% analysis of base glaze:
SiO_2 59.45; Al_2O_3 24.77; FeO 0.05; CaO 1.45; K_2O 2.68; Na_2O 9.09; Li_2O 2.51

SHI 4. Malcolm shino, cone 9–10 (from Malcolm Davis).

Kona F4 soda feldspar	11.0
Nepheline syenite	45.0
China clay	10.0
Ball clay	15.0
Soda ash	19.0
	100.0

% analysis of base glaze:
SiO_2 49.66; TiO_2 0.24; Al_2O_3 20.68; FeO 0.16; CaO 0.54; MgO 0.09; K_2O 2.99; Na_2O 25.64

Potter's notes: The origin of 'Meyer' in SHI3 is unknown, but SHI4 is attributed to Malcolm Davis. Both are cone 9 to 10 glazes although they are shown here from a 24-hour wood firing to cone 13 in a 2.8 m^3 (100 cu. ft) mountain climbing kiln. From a 5am start there is a slow heat-up

with ash deposition until 6pm when cone 012 goes over. At 7pm heavy reduction for 1 hour with reduction maintained until 2am when the kiln reaches cone 10. This is followed by a 3-hour soak to melt all the ash.

Lowering the maturing range of shino glazes.

Adding a high alkaline frit (such as Ferro F3110) to a shino that is too matt will bring about a better melt. Tests adding 5%, 10% and 15% of the frit are usually effective in finding a brighter glaze.

The high silica glazes

Juns

'Jun' glazes are characterised by a bluish opalescence that can range from just a hint of suffused pale blue colour, through whitish blue spots and streaks within a transparent glaze to a virtually opaque white glaze. A small percentage of reduced iron seems to be essential and can be provided either as a glaze ingredient or indirectly from an underlying iron-bearing body or slip. The colour and opacity is an optical effect in which colloidal particles

scatter light from the blue end of the spectrum and Jun glazes need to be applied quite thickly for the colour to develop.

There are four main routes to creating a Jun opalescence:
- Low alumina, high silica glazes
- Titanium dioxide
- Phosphorous pentoxide
- Boric oxide

The low alumina Juns

JUN 1 and JUN 2 are glazes nos. 40 and 47 from the set of tests (see p.24) used for exploring the whereabouts of transparent glazes. The low alumina content of the glaze means that all of the alumina will be taken up in glaze formation and that the other two components – fluxes and silica – will remain outside of the glass structure. This position, with the SiO_2 at 65–70% and the Al_2O_3 at 5–10%, must create the right condition for the nucleation of crystals that will scatter light at this wavelength. The more opaque glazes also arise from undissolved silica.

JUN 1. Cone 9–11 (from the author).

Nepheline syenite	17.5
China clay	6.0
Dolomite	27.7
Whiting	6.5
Quartz	42.3
	100.0

% analysis of base glaze:
SiO_2 66.79; Al_2O_3 7.35; CaO 15.13; MgO 7.25; FeO 0.08; K_2O 1.22; Na_2O 2.18

Potter's notes: These two tests tiles are the same glaze – yet another illustration of the vagaries that are set to confound potters! The difference is that the Jun-like glaze (on the left) has been fired over a terracotta clay slip and it may also have been in a hotter part of the kiln.

JUN 2. Cone 9–11 (from the author).

Nepheline syenite	18.1
Dolomite	30.2
Whiting	7.3
Quartz	44.4
	100.0

% analysis of base glaze:
SiO_2 66.85; Al_2O_3 5.03; CaO 16.79; MgO 7.98; FeO 0.03; K_2O 1.09; Na_2O 2.23

JUN 1 over red clay slip (left) and on a buff body (right).

Potter's notes: Being further away than JUN 1 from the transparent glaze area, this is a more opaque glaze.

JUN 3. Cone 9 (from Matthew Waite). Original glaze recipe attributed to Derek Emms and published in *The Potter's Dictionary of Materials and Techniques* by Frank and Janet Hamer. Although this recipe contains colemanite, it is a small amount, and relates more to this low alumina Jun rather than the boric oxide section. Its position on the graph $SiO_2:Al_2O_3$ 68%:9% places it just below the main transparent area.

Potash feldspar	44.0
Colemanite	1.0
China clay	1.0
Talc	4.0
Whiting	20.0
Quartz	30.0
	100.0
Black iron oxide	1.0

% analysis of base glaze:
SiO_2 68.27; Al_2O_3 9.40; B_2O_3 0.49; CaO 12.86; MgO 1.44; FeO 0.07; K_2O 6.05; Na_2O 1.42

Bottle vase by Matthew Waite, using JUN 3 over a buff clay, with tenmoku rim.

Potter's notes: Jun needs to be applied thickly and is best at the top (hotter) part of my cone 9 firing.

The titanium dioxide Juns

This is one of the least problematic methods for creating a Jun glaze. A small test series putting between 2% and 8% of titanium dioxide (TiO_2) into any transparent glaze will yield a Jun. Rutile or ilmenite (minerals that combine TiO_2 and iron) are also often used as a source.

JUN 4. Opal blue glaze, cone 9–10 (from John Harlow).

Nepheline syenite	36.8
China clay	5.3
Ball clay Hymod AT	5.3
Dolomite	15.8
Whiting	3.2
Zinc oxide	3.2
Flint/quartz	30.4
	100.0
Rutile	5.1

JUN 2 over a red clay slip.

Test tile of JUN 4 by John Harlow.

JUN 5 on jug by Douglas Phillips.

% analysis of base glaze:
SiO_2 64.67; TiO_2 0.07; Al_2O_3 13.60; FeO 0.15; ZnO 3.56; CaO 7.91; MgO 3.91; K_2O 2.07; Na_2O 4.04

Potter's notes: Reduced from cone 07 onwards with a 20 minute soak. Firing time approximately 11 hours. I prefer it over a white clay but mostly use it as an overlay – especially over tenmokus.

JUN 5. *Blue Jun glaze, cone 10 (from Douglas Phillips).*
White to strong blue with green fleck, bleeds clear on rims and handle edges.

FFF potash feldspar	27.0
Local clay	25.0
Ball clay (high silica)	12.4
Dolomite	10.4
Whiting	7.4
Quartz	17.8
	100.0
Rutile	5.5

% analysis of base glaze:
SiO_2 66.45; TiO_2 0.35; P_2O_5 0.04; Al_2O_3 12.66; CaO 10.33; MgO 3.38; FeO 1.46; K_2O 3.46; Na_2O 1.87

Potter's notes: We use this glaze both on bisque and as a raw glaze on dry pots. It is sensitive to clay body, thickness and firing.

The phosphorous pentoxide Juns

Phosphorous pentoxide (P_2O_5) can be introduced as bone ash or may be found in some, but not all, wood ashes. Some potters add around 5% of bone ash to their wood ash to help get the Jun effect.

JUN 6 on a small bowl by Malcolm Jepson.

JUN 6. Cone 10+ (from Malcolm Jepson).

Potash feldspar	40.0
Mixed wood ash	33.3
Quartz	26.7
	100.0

Approximate % analysis of JUN6 using a generic wood ash:
SiO_2 66; P_2O_5 1; Al_2O_3 11; CaO 10; MgO 1; FeO 1; K_2O 6; Na_2O 3; other oxides (traces) 1

Potter's notes: Used over a red clay slip. Although most of my work is raw fired, the slip traps carbonates within the body. This causes bloating and pots using this slip/glaze combination need to be bisque fired. The glaze must be applied thickly. In tests, better blues came from using quartz rather than flint as a source of silica.

The boron Juns

These Juns too are found in glazes that are rather low in alumina. They seem to be quite difficult to get right but their devotees show admirable persistence. The main problem with sources of boric oxide is solubility so the glazes don't keep well in slop form.

JUN 7.Cone 10–11 (from Michael Gaitskell).

FFF potash feldspar	39.6
Calcium borate frit	5.0
China clay	2.0
Bentonite	0.5
Dolomite	9.9
Whiting	7.9
Flint	34.6
Bone ash	0.5
	100.0
Red iron oxide	1.8

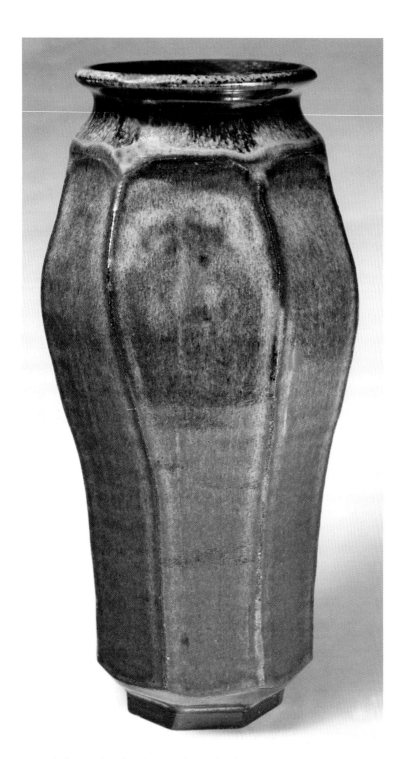

Cut-sided vase glazed with JUN 7 by Michael Gaitskell.

% analysis of base glaze:
SiO_2 69.15; P_2O_5 0.30; Al_2O_3 9.37;
B_2O_3 2.74; CaO 10.44; MgO 2.38;
K_2O 3.28; Na_2O 2.26

Potter's notes: This can be an elusive glaze but at its best the opalescence comes from a suspension of sinewy, smoky trails within a transparent, glassy glaze. The typical length of firing is 12–14 hours. Reduction begins at 980°C–1000°C (1796°F–1832°F) with a 20-minute soak at top temperature – cone 10 over and cone 11 bending. Relatively quick cool to 1000°C (1832°F) then clammed and cooled over two days.

Nuka

'Nuka' refers originally to the Japanese glazes containing the high silica ingredient: rice husk. They come within the same opaque, low alumina: low flux: high silica area as the Chinese Jun glazes but may lack the blue opalescence.

JUN 8. 'Reconstructed' Nuka, cone 9 (from Matthew Waite).

Potash feldspar	36.0
Bone ash	2.0
High alkaline frit	3.0
Hyplas 71 (a high silica ball clay)	6.0
Talc	2.0
Whiting	21.0
Quartz	30.0
	100.0
Black iron oxide	1.0

% analysis of base glaze:
SiO_2 67.03; TiO_2 0.11; P_2O_5 1.02;
Al_2O_3 8.90; B_2O_3 0.13; CaO 14.58; MgO 0.74; FeO 0.09; K_2O 5.64; Na_2O 1.76

Potter's notes: This is called a 'reconstructed' Nuka. The original recipe came from *Ash Glazes* by Phil Rogers. As with JUN 3

Small bottle with a single lug by Matthew Waite using JUN 8 over a buff crank clay. The pink/purple blush is a copper flashing from an adjacent pot in the kiln.

this needs to be applied thickly and is best at the top (hotter) part of my cone 9 firing.

Summary for the low iron glazes

The glazes from the last three sections, based on 1. high alkaline glazes, 2. high alumina glazes and 3. high silica glazes, are plotted on the graph (see p.70) in relation to the transparent glaze area. Even though we are dealing with glazes supplied by many potters and all the variables that this implies – different clays, materials and firings – a consistent pattern can be seen. In practice there is no exact dividing line between the different glaze types and one area grades into another.

For potters working with a single clay body, a specific set of glaze-making ingredients and a repeatable firing regime, it is possible to bring these variables under much tighter control. Plotting glazes, even in this very simple way, can be particularly useful in seeing how glazes may be modified to adjust for transparency versus opacity and for shiny, satin and matt finishes.

Bowl by Matthew Waite showing JUN 8 over a black slip (Hyplas 71 ball clay 80% + black iron oxide 10% and manganese dioxide 10%).

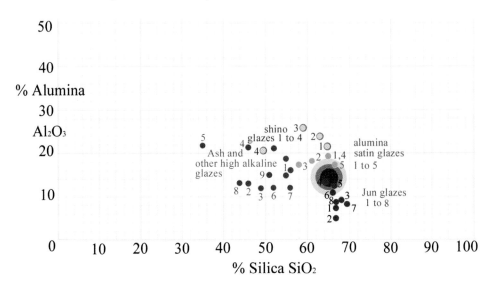

(Fig. 10) Plotting **1**. the high alkaline and 'ash' glazes (purple) **2**. the high alumina satin (green) and shino glaze (yellow) and **3**. the high silica Jun and Nuka glazes (blue). The main transparent area falls within the red circle.

Chapter Six
The high iron glazes

Tenmokus – black breaking to rust

Tenmokus are dark brown to black, satin to shiny, iron-rich glazes. One very popular version is a shiny satin, virtually opaque deep black that breaks to brown where the glaze is thinner. This 'break' may be on the edge of fluted sections, handles and rims which helps to emphasise and define the form. The difference that shows up between a 'thin' brown and a 'thick' black application can also be used to advantage to reflect the way the work was glazed, capturing something of the liveliness and spontaneity of poured glazing techniques.

Finding a black tenmoku

All tenmoku glazes contain iron oxide – typically somewhere around 5–8% of the chemical analysis – but not all base glazes make suitable vehicles for producing tenmokus. Searching for a black tenmoku by adding red iron oxide to the 1–49 set of plain base glazes given on pp.23–4 is a very good example of the usefulness of

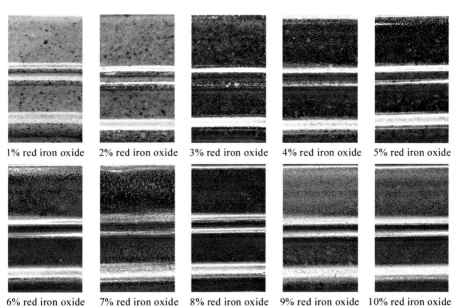

1% red iron oxide 2% red iron oxide 3% red iron oxide 4% red iron oxide 5% red iron oxide

6% red iron oxide 7% red iron oxide 8% red iron oxide 9% red iron oxide 10% red iron oxide

A progression test showing 1% increments of red iron oxide added to base test no. 20, fired to cone 9 on a buff body. Recipe: nepheline syenite 12.8; china clay 26.6, dolomite 15.7; whiting 2.9; quartz 42.1.

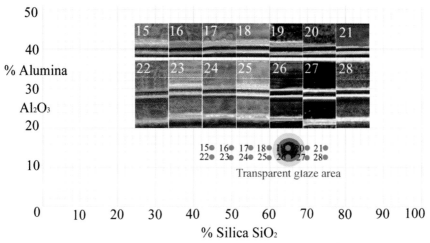

50

40

% Alumina

30

Al₂O₃

20

10

0

| 10 | 20 | 30 | 40 | 50 | 60 | 70 | 80 | 90 | 100 |

% Silica SiO₂

15● 16● 17● 18● 19●20● 21●
22● 23● 24● 25● 26●27● 28●

Transparent glaze area

(Fig. 11) Blue dots: the Al₂O₃:SiO₂ position of base glazes 15–28 from p.23. Inset: photographs of tests 15–28 with the addition of 5% red iron oxide. Clearly, out of the entire 49 glazes, only one base glaze, no. 27, stands out as being a candidate base glaze for this type of tenmoku.

plotting the Al₂O₃:SiO₂ ratio for homing in on a particular glaze. But how much iron should one add? A very helpful test when trying out any tenmoku recipe is a simple progression in which increasing amounts of red iron oxide are added to the base glaze. For example, using test no. 20 from this set, the experiment starts with 1% of red iron oxide being added to the glaze. This is then sieved and the test tile dipped in a manner that replicates, as far as possible, one's normal glazing thickness. This process is simply repeated, adding another 1% of red iron oxide, then sieving and dipping – in this case stopping at the 10% addition (shown on p.71).

The progression on this buff body goes from a celadon at 2% to dark green at 3% and 4%. The nearest to a tenmoku is the black-brown slightly mottled glaze at only 5% and from 6% onwards the glazes enter the iron red range. Many of the recipes that follow in this chapter call for 7% of red iron oxide and it is fair to say that, used over this fairly high iron, buff firing clay, they would all have missed the black variation and come out

in the iron brown range. Therefore it pays to do this very simple progression test and find out just how much iron oxide is needed for your clay and firing.

Based on the above test, 5% red iron oxide has been added to the 49 tests used in Chapter Five (pp. 23–24) to see if there is also a 'best' position for a tenmoku. The graph above shows the result of adding 5% red iron oxide to the tests 15–28, fired to cone 9 on a buff

TEN 1. Black tenmoku (5% red iron oxide in test no.27).

Jug by the author using TEN 2 over red clay slip with sgraffito decoration.

clay. These base recipes are along the 12.5% and 15% Al_2O_3 line and were the only rows to produce black tenmokus.

TEN 1. *Black tenmoku (based on test no.27).*

Nepheline syenite	14.4
China clay	19.9
Dolomite	18.3
Whiting	3.5
Flint/quartz	43.9
	100.0

Red iron oxide	5.0

% analysis of base glaze:
SiO_2 71.13; TiO_2 0.02; Al_2O_3 11.82; FeO 0.19; CaO 9.07; MgO 4.57; K_2O 1.37; Na_2O 1.83

Potter's notes: Used over a white clay, the red iron oxide may need to be increased by 1–2%.

The following tenmoku recipes have much in common with TEN 1, using feldspars, clay, the alkaline earths (dolomite and whiting) and silica (flint or quartz).

TEN 2. *Black tenmoku, cone 9–10 (from the author).*

Cornish stone	65.4
China clay	7.7
Whiting	11.5
Flint/quartz	15.4
	100.0

Red iron oxide	7.0

% analysis of base glaze:
SiO_2 71.50; TiO_2 0.05; P_2O_5 0.35; Al_2O_3 14.50; FeO 0.10; CaO 8.29; K_2O 2.60; Na_2O 2.61

Potter's notes: A reliable tenmoku from a recipe published by John Maltby.

TEN 3 on two porcelain teapots by Melanie Brown. The gold lustre decoration has been fired on in a separate low-temperature firing.

Faceted bowl by Margaret Frith, using TEN 4.

TEN 3. *Black tenmoku, cone 9–10 (from Melanie Brown).*

Potash feldspar	44.0
Standard borax frit	7.0
China clay	15.0
Dolomite	7.0
Whiting	7.0
Flint/quartz	20.0
	100.0
Red iron oxide	7.0

% analysis of base glaze:
SiO_2 64.73; Al_2O_3 15.93; B_2O_3 1.44; FeO 0.04; CaO 8.07; MgO 1.68; K_2O 6.05; Na_2O 2.06

Potter's notes: Super reliable. I use this glaze to fill up the cool spots in the kiln. It has a wide firing range and is very stable. It is equally good on porcelain or stoneware. Fired with a steady reduction from cone 04 until cone 10 starts to bend, then off and clam up.

TEN 4. *Cone 9+ (from Margaret Frith).*

Potash feldspar	77.2
High silica ball clay	10.6
Whiting	9.0
Flint/quartz	3.2
	100.0
Red iron oxide	7.9

% analysis of base glaze:
SiO2 64.20; TiO_2 0.19; Al_2O_3 17.18;
FeO 0.15; CaO 5.61; MgO 0.05;
K_2O 10.23; Na_2O 2.39

TEN 5. *Black tenmoku, cone 10–11 (from Michael Gaitskell).*

FFF potash feldspar	31.6
China clay	15.8
Whiting	17.2
Flint/quartz	35.4
	100.0
Red iron oxide	7.5

% analysis of base glaze:
SiO_2 70.76; P_2O_5 0.04; Al_2O_3 13.32;
FeO 0.17; CaO 10.73; K_2O 2.88;
Na_2O 2.10

Round vase by Michael Gaitskell, using TEN 5.

Potter's notes: At the correct thickness this user-friendly glaze breaks to nut brown on ridges and rims. Fired in reduction from cone 06 onwards with a 20-minute soak to cone 10 over and cone 11 bending.

TEN 6. Black tenmoku, cone 10 (from Paul Green).

Cornish stone	39.0
FFF potash feldspar	17.0
China clay	7.5
Whiting	16.5
Flint/quartz	20.0
	100.0
Red iron oxide	8.5

% analysis of base glaze:
SiO_2 69.60; TiO_2 0.03; P_2O_5 0.22; Al_2O3 13.32; FeO 0.06; CaO 10.95; MgO 0.06; K_2O 3.31; Na_2O 2.45

Potter's notes: Years ago I used a Russell Collins glaze from *Ceramic Review Book of Clay and Glaze Recipes.* This used 3% iron spangles, as well as the 5.5% red iron, I eventually abandoned the spangles and made some adjustments to the quantities of the other materials. The firing is slowed down between 800°C–1000°C (1472°F–1832°F) before reduction begins to burn out carbonaceous material in the clay, with a soak at the top end from cone 9 bending to cone 10 down. No difference noted in this glaze if the kiln is clammed up immediately at the end of the firing or after a fast cool down to 1000°C (1832°F).

TEN 7. Black tenmoku, cone 9–10 (from Christine McCole and Roger Brann).

Soda feldspar	25.0
HV ball clay	25.0
Whiting	20.0
Flint	15.0
Quartz	15.0
	100.0
Red iron oxide	10.0

% analysis of base glaze:
SiO_2 70.17; TiO_2 0.44; Al_2O_3 12.53; FeO 0.25; CaO 12.81; MgO 0.09; K_2O 1.49; Na2O 2.22

Potter's notes: A dark red-black tenmoku, breaking on rims and incised decoration. As a raw glaze it has a tendency to crawl and crack on rims so is mainly used on bisque-fired ware. We can, however, use it for single firing on the inside of pots such as baking dishes.

Tenmoku jug by Paul Green, using TEN 6.

Wood-fired tenmoku (TEN 7) on casserole by Christine McCole and Roger Brann (Hafod Hill Pottery).

TEN 8. *Black tenmoku, cone 10–11 (from 'Made in Cley').*

Potash feldspar	60.0
China clay	5.0
Whiting	10.0
Flint/quartz	25.0
	100.0

Red iron oxide	7.0

% analysis of base glaze:
SiO_2 70.36; Al_2O_3 13.77; FeO 0.05; CaO 6.15; K_2O 7.84; Na_2O 1.83

Potter's notes: Thickness of glaze is fairly critical, try to get a medium coating. The firing takes 15 hours with reduction starting at cone 06. The kiln's temperature rises so slowly towards the end of the firing cycle that it is effectively a soak and we finish with a 10-minute re-oxidation period when cone 11 is starting to bend. The dampers are closed immediately at the end of the firing.

TEN 9. *Black tenmoku, cone 6–7 (from Marcia Selsor).*

Soda feldspar Kona F4	55.8
China clay EPK	6.6
Whiting	12.0
Flint/quartz	25.6
	100.0

Manganese dioxide	2.6
Red iron oxide	10.0

% analysis of base glaze:
SiO_2 70.37; P_2O5 0.02; Al_2O_3 14.35; FeO 0.05; CaO 8.20; K_2O 2.89; Na_2O 4.12

Potter's notes: Reduction starts at cone 09, then light to neutral up to cone 6 with a 45-minute soak of heavier reduction.

TEN 8. Tenmoku dish by 'Made in Cley'. *Photograph from Richard Kelham.*

TEN 9. Mug by Marcia Selsor.

TEN 10. Black tenmoku vase by Matthew Waite.

TEN 10. *Black tenmoku, cone 9 (from Matthew Waite).*

Potash feldspar	65.0
China clay	8.0
Whiting	12.0
Flint/quartz	15.0
	100.0

Red iron oxide	8.0

% analysis of base glaze:
SiO_2 65.65; Al_2O_3 16.21; FeO 0.06;
CaO 7.46; K_2O 8.61; Na_2O 2.01

Potter's notes: This tenmoku came from a recipe supplied by Roger Harris in *Ceramic Review*, no. 180. The vase was glazed on the inside and on the rim with Nuka (see p.69). The tenmoku was poured on downwards over the shoulder and the rim and neck, then dipped in tenmoku over the Nuka. Fired in reduction from cone 07 with a steady climb to cone 9 bending.

The next three glazes are still in the black tenmoku arena but introduce some different fluxes and colouring oxides.

TEN 11. Porcelain bowl with Hamada rust tenmoku by John Britt.

Jug by John Harlow with TEN 12 (top half) overlapping a buff glaze.

Thrown, altered and assembled stem-cup by John Britt. TEN 13 with paper resist circles on the bowl. COPR 2 (see p.96) on the stem, handle and inside bowl.

TEN 11. *Hamada rust tenmoku, cone 9–10 (from John Britt).*

Custer (potash) feldspar	77.0
China clay	4.3
Gerstley borate	12.4
Whiting	6.2
Flint/quartz	0.1
	100.0
Red iron oxide	7.0

% analysis of base glaze:
SiO_2 61.61; Al_2O_3 16.99; B_2O_3 3.61; FeO 0.10; CaO 6.49; K_2O 8.42; Na_2O 2.78

Potter's notes: This is a high alkaline, low alumina tenmoku. It is very runny. You have to apply it very carefully. If you fire it too fast between 204°C–482°C (400°F–900°F) it will butterfly roll off (crawl), because the Gerstley borate releases chemical water too quickly. 5–8% red iron oxide will give variations of tenmoku. Fired with reduction from cone 06 to cone 9 bending, with a 10 minute oxidation period to finish. Natural cool.

TEN 12. *Cone 9–10 (from John Harlow).*

FFF potash feldspar	40.5
China clay	6.4
AT ball clay	5.3
Barium carbonate	10.6
Whiting	10.6
Zinc oxide	5.3
Flint/quartz	21.3
	100.0
Ilmenite	6.0

% analysis of base glaze:
SiO_2 59.39; Al_2O_3 12.80; TiO_2 0.07; P_2O_5 0.06; FeO 0.16; BaO 8.97; CaO 6.90; MgO 0.02; ZnO 5.79; K_2O 3.50; Na_2O 2.34

Potter's notes: The original glaze came from Lasse Ostman's website and is probably the most versatile glaze I have used. A superb base glaze for over-laying other glazes, really well-behaved and forgiving. On its own a classic tenmoku breaking to rust on the edges. At higher temperatures develops flecks of gold.

TEN 13. Candace Black, cone 9–10 (from John Britt).

Kona F4 soda feldspar	65.0
EPK china clay	5.0
Dolomite	5.0
Whiting	5.0
Flint/quartz	20.0
	100.0
Cobalt carbonate	5.0
Red iron oxide	8.0

% analysis of base glaze:
SiO_2 67.87; P_2O_5 0.01; Al_2O_3, 15.11; FeO 0.04; CaO 7.96; MgO 1.13; K_2O 3.24; Na_2O 4.64

Tea-dust tenmokus

The name 'tea-dust', for this type of tenmoku, describes the scattering of matt, yellow to green speckles (the 'tea-dust') in a high iron glaze. Looking at their Al_2O_3:SiO_2 position on the graph they are found just below the main transparent area. Here, for example, is test tile no. 40 plus 5% red iron oxide from the set used in Chapter Five (see p. 24). It shows the micro-crystalline development that is to be found in this type of glaze.

Being relatively low in alumina, we can understand that all of the Al_2O_3 will be taken up in glass formation, leaving an excess of fluxes and silica. The fluxes, in particular the calcium and magnesium oxides, will combine with the silica to form a group of crystals called pyroxenes. The amount of specking can therefore be controlled in a glaze containing approximately 65% silica, by altering the amount of alumina in the recipe. In TEA1, for example, adding an extra 5% of china clay will reduce the specking because it will head the glaze back towards the transparent area. Conversely, reducing the china clay will have the opposite effect, unbalancing it even further and allowing more crystal growth.

Tea-dust tenmoku test tile.

TEA 1. *Tea-dust tenmoku, cone 9–10 (from the author).*

Potash feldspar	18.0
China clay	9.5
Dolomite	21.0
Whiting	12.5
Flint/quartz	39.0
	100.0

Red iron oxide	7.0

% analysis of base glaze:
SiO_2 66.20; Al_2O_3 8.48; FeO 0.02; CaO 16.49; MgO 5.51; K_2O 2.67; Na_2O 0.63

Oil-spot and hare's-fur tenmokus

These are related and rather difficult glazes that require the right firing and glazing conditions before they will work properly. Both need to be applied thickly. The spots and streaks are formed by bubbles in the glaze as it begins to melt and the firing needs to stop at the point when these have healed over but have not disappeared. Glaze no.4 from the 1–49 transparent tests (pp.23–24) produced this oil-spot glaze with the addition of 8% red iron oxide.

Detail of oil-spot glaze OIL 1.

OIL 1. *Oil-spot tenmoku, cone 9–10 (from the author).*

Nepheline syenite	19.6
China clay	32.2
Dolomite	20.1
Whiting	3.1
Flint/quartz	25.0
	100.0

Red iron oxide	8.0

% analysis of base glaze:
SiO_2 61.50; TiO_2 0.04; Al_2O_3 18.60; FeO 0.30; CaO 9.76; MgO 5.15; K_2O 2.05; Na_2O 2.60

None of the high-iron glazes are solely reliant on reduction. On the contrary, many fine tenmokus and allied glazes can be fired in oxidation as, for example, these two oil-spots by John Britt. It has to be remembered that in a reduction firing the iron oxide Fe_2O_3 converts to FeO and essentially behaves as a flux. In oxidised firing, the red iron oxide remains as Fe_2O_3 and has an effect that is more akin to adding alumina. This means that the plain base recipe used to make a particular high iron reduction glaze will not necessarily be the right starting point for an oxidised equivalent.

OIL 2. *Oil-spot tenmoku, oxidised, cone 8–9 (from John Britt).*

F-4 soda feldspar	48.0
China clay	9.6
Dolomite	3.7
Whiting	3.7
Flint/quartz	35.0
	100.0

Red iron oxide	8.0
Cobalt carbonate	5.0

% analysis of base glaze:
SiO_2 75.11; Al_2O_3 13.87; Fe_2O_3 0.01; CaO 4.26; MgO 0.85; K_2O 2.42; Na_2O 3.48

Jug with TEA 1, tea-dust tenmoku, by the author.

Mug by John Britt using the oil-spot glaze (OIL 2), fired in oxidation.

Detail of bowl using oil-spot glaze (OIL 3) by John Britt. Oxidised firing.

Detail of hare's-fur HAR 1.

Test tile showing IROR 1.

OIL 3. *Oil-spot tenmoku, oxidised, cone 8–9 (from John Britt).*

Potash feldspar	25.0
F-4 soda feldspar	35.0
Ferro frit F3110	5.0
China clay	15.0
Dolomite	5.0
Talc	5.0
Flint/quartz	8.0
Bentonite	2.0
	100.0
Red iron oxide	6.0

% analysis of base glaze:
SiO_2 66.55; TiO_2 0.02; Al_2O_3 18.08; B_2O_3 0.14; Fe_2O_3 0.27; CaO 2.77; MgO 2.84; K_2O 4.84; Na_2O 4.49

Potter's notes for OIL 2 and OIL 3: Fired in full oxidation throughout the firing. You can watch the pieces start bubbling up and stop the kiln when the glazes smooth over. Sometimes I will re-fire pieces that are not smooth. Glaze application is critical. It must be thick. I use three dips.

In comparison with the shiny tenmokus, the oil-spot and hare's-fur glazes are found in the satin to matt range. For example,

glaze no. 3 from the 1–49 transparent tests (pp. 23–24) produced this hare's-fur glaze with the addition of 8% red iron oxide.

HAR 1. *Hare's-fur, cone 9–10 (from author).*

Nepheline syenite	24.4
China clay	28.4
Dolomite	24.9
Whiting	3.8
Flint/quartz	18.5
	100.0
Red iron oxide	7.0

% analysis of base glaze:
SiO_2 56.50; TiO_2 0.03; Al_2O_3 18.78; FeO 0.28; CaO 12.37; MgO 6.54; K_2O 2.28; Na_2O 3.22

The iron reds

Our line test at the beginning of this section (p. 71) showed how the progressive increase of red iron oxide yielded celadons, then tenmokus, and then iron-red glazes that became increasingly saturated and metallic. As a rule of thumb, adding a further 2% of red iron oxide to a black tenmoku will produce an iron red. Iron reds can also be achieved by putting a celadon or tenmoku over an iron-

Raw-glazed dish with IROR 2 by Roger Brann and Christine McCole (Hafod Hill Pottery).

bearing slip (e.g., as on the lower half of the jug showing TEN 2 on p.74).

IROR 1. *Variegated iron red, cone 9–10 (from the author).*

Nepheline syenite	15.8
China clay	24.0
Dolomite	20.2
Whiting	4.0
Flint/quartz	36.0
	100.0
Red iron oxide	8.0

% analysis of base glaze:
SiO_2 66.57; TiO_2 0.03; Al_2O_3 14.10; FeO 0.22; CaO 10.28; MgO 5.14; K_2O 1.59; Na_2O 2.07

IROR 2. *Hafod Hill Pottery's raw-glazed iron red, cone 10.*

Soda feldspar	25.0
Ball clay HVAR	25.0
Bone ash	10.0
Dolomite	15.0
Flint/quartz	25.0
	100.0
Red iron oxide	10.0

% analysis of base glaze:
SiO_2 63.50; TiO_2 0.43; P_2O_5 4.57; Al_2O_3 12.34; FeO 0.25; CaO 11.45; MgO 3.74; K_2O 1.50; Na_2O 2.22

Potter's notes: A red/brown, sometimes plum coloured glaze. Used thickly (double cream) on leatherhard pots. This is very reliable, with quite a wide-firing range of cone 9 to 11.

Another variety of iron reds involves the rather remarkable reaction between irons in recipes containing bone ash and lithia.

IROR 3. *Orange-red, cone 6 and 9 (from Christine and Peter Penfold).*

	Cone 6	Cone 9
Potash feldspar	46.7	44.0
China clay	4.0	8.5
Bentonite	2.0	1.5
Bone ash	15.0	12.0
Lithium carbonate	4.0	4.0
Talc	16.9	10.0
Flint/quartz	11.4	20.0
	100.0	100.0
Red iron oxide	11.5	8.5

% analysis of base glaze cone 6 version:
SiO_2 57.68; TiO_2 0.01; P_2O_5 7.16; Al_2O_3 11.12; FeO 0.23; CaO 8.84; MgO 5.69; K_2O 6.14; Na_2O 1.44; Li_2O 1.69

% analysis of base glaze cone 9 version:
SiO_2 62.46; TiO_2 0.01; P_2O_5 5.74; Al_2O_3 12.34; FeO 0.17; CaO 7.08; MgO 3.38; K_2O 5.77; Na_2O 1.35; Li_2O 1.70

Potter's notes: A strong colour which breaks into an attractive dark olive. Fires at 200°C (392°F) per hour to the start of reduction at cone 06. Then approximately 2½ hours to cone 9. It is well worth testing the amount of red iron oxide in the recipe. Between 6% to 12% you will find most variations.

Plate by Christine and Peter Penfold using the cone 9 version of IROR 3.

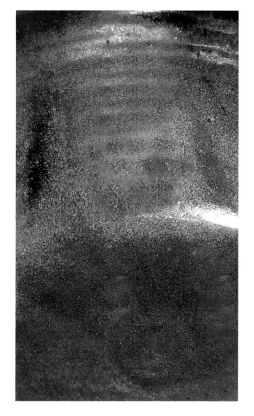

Detail of bowl by Marcia Selsor, showing IROR 4.

IROR 4. Ohata red, cone 6–7
(from Marcia Selsor).

Potash feldspar	52.0
Gerstley borate	4.0
China clay	6.0
Bone ash	14.0
Lithium carbonate	4.0
Dolomite	8.0
Flint/quartz	12.0
	100.0
Red iron oxide	8.0

% analysis of base glaze:
SiO_2 53.98; TiO_2 0.01; P_2O_5 6.89;
Al_2O_3 12.62; B_2O_3 1.18; FeO 0.06;
CaO 11.9; MgO 1.88; K_2O 5.86;
Na_2O 1.87; Li_2O 1.75

Potter's notes: A high-iron glaze with colour variations from brown, through red to dark mauve.

Kaki tenmokus

'Kaki' is derived from the Japanese name for and colour of the persimmon fruit. The base glazes for the kaki type are found to be comparatively high in silica and alumina. They are often used as over-glazes, in which case calcining some of the clay content is usually recommended.

KAK 1. Kaki over-glaze, cone 10 (from David Frith).

Potash feldspar	32.5
China clay	21.6
Dolomite	6.5
Whiting	1.6
Quartz	37.8
	100.0
Red iron oxide	7.0
Titanium dioxide	1.1

% analysis of base glaze:
SiO_2 74.37; TiO_2 0.02; Al_2O_3 14.57;
FeO 0.19; CaO 3.31; MgO 1.52;
K_2O 4.85; Na_2O 1.17

Lidded box by David Frith, with KAK 1 over-glaze using wax-resist decoration.

Bowl by David Winkley. KAK 2 over blue celadon with wax-resist decoration. (KAK 2 is also shown over the celadon CEL 8 glaze on p. 36.)

KAK 2. *Kaki iron overglaze, cone 10–11 (from David Winkley).*
An iron glaze, unprepossessing by itself, which becomes rich and variegated if used over other suitable glazes. Excellent with wax-resist where it imparts a dark defining edge to brushwork.

Cornish stone	54.2
Ball clay Hyplas 71	11.8
Calcined ball clay BLU	12.8
(previously called TWVD)	
Talc	5.9
Wollastonite	5.4
Flint	9.9
	100.0
Red iron oxide	6.0

% analysis of base glaze:
SiO_2 74.96; TiO_2 0.28; P_2O_5 0.30; Al_2O_3 12.53; FeO 0.21; CaO 4.04; MgO 2.35; K_2O 3.09; Na_2O 2.24

Potter's notes: The ball clay is calcined to cone 07 and the glaze batch is ball-milled for 3 hours. It needs good reduction and heat above cone 10 is best. Its quality seems to depend on the underneath glaze melting just before the top glaze; it is gradually drawn down into the melt as the glaze matures. Wollastonite is a very alkaline material and its inclusion in a recipe can result in the glaze settling very hard in the bottom of the container. Adding a small amount of vinegar (i.e. a teaspoon

Fluted bowl by John Leach using KAK 3 beneath an opaque overglaze.

per gallon) may help, or up to 2% bentonite as a suspender or both.

KAK 3. *John Leach's Kaki underglaze, cone 9–11.*

Cornish stone	70.0
HV ball clay	20.0
(previously called HVAR)	
Whiting	10.0
	100.0
Red iron oxide	7.5

% analysis of base glaze:
SiO_2 68.35; TiO_2 0.39; P_2O_5 0.35; Al_2O_3 16.97; FeO 0.27; CaO 7.07; MgO 0.16; K_2O 8.82; Na_2O 2.61

KAK 3A. *Opaque overglaze, cone 9–11 (from John Leach).*

Cornish stone	80.0
HV Ball clay	10.0
(previously called HVAR)	
Whiting	10.0
	100.0

Potter's notes: The above combination is good for sgraffito and wax-resist decoration. We fire in a 9.9 m^3 (350 cu. ft) three-chambered Noborigama kiln. Reduction starts at 860°C (1580°F) with a soak for 2 to 3 hours at top temperature.

Test tile of HAE 1 plus 8% red iron oxide.

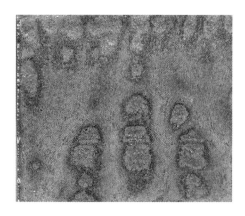

High-iron 'ash' type glazes

The final task in this section is to look at the high alkaline area that produces the 'wood-ash' type of glazes. The iron colouring tends to be rather muted and the surface develops a typical mottled and streaked appearance. For example, here is HAE 1, a high alkaline earth, variegated, mottled, black-brown satin glaze.

HAE 1. Cone 9–10 (from the author).

Nepheline syenite	19.3
China clay	9.5
Dolomite	22.3
Whiting	20.0
Flint/quartz	<u>28.9</u>
	100.0
Red iron oxide	8.0

% analysis of base glaze:
SiO_2 56.72; Al_2O_3 10.34; FeO 0.03;
CaO 23.05; MgO 6.14; K_2O 1.22;
Na_2O 2.50

BELOW: **(Fig. 11a)** Graph showing the alumina: silica ratios for various tenmoku glazes.

The high-iron glazes – an overview

The graph below highlights those regions on the Al_2O_3: SiO_2 graph where the various types of high iron glazes are to be found. This can be a great help in finding and adjusting particular glazes and can hopefully save the potter a great deal of time and wasted effort. For example, if you are interested in oil-spot or hare's-fur glazes, they will only be found in this higher alumina and lower silica position. Admittedly the other variables: the clay, the glaze application and the firing, will all play their part. Success may not be guaranteed with this system but testing in the right spot will certainly help!

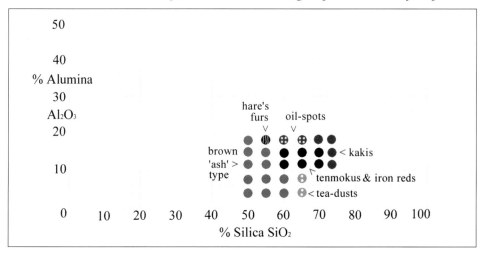

Chapter Seven
Copper glazes

Copper in glazes is a real turncoat and can produce all sorts of blues, greens, pinks and reds, actual metallic coppery gold lustres, or even virtually no colour at all. This depends upon:
- the kiln atmosphere at various stages in the firing cycle
- the base glaze
- and the underlying clay body or slip

Copper reds

The red in copper reds comes from minute particles of colloidal copper (Cu) within the glaze. This is described as a state that is midway between being dissolved in solution and a solid in suspension. A few recipes use black copper oxide but most favour using copper carbonate, as this seems to give a better dispersal. In any event the copper carbonate will have decomposed by 500°C (932°F), giving off carbon dioxide and leaving copper oxide behind. (If you peep into the kiln early in the firing, glazes that contained the green powdered copper carbonate will have turned a pale grey.)

$$CuCO_3 > CuO + CO_2\char`\^$$

The brightest reds come from less than 0.5% copper, with typical amounts of around 0.3% copper carbonate being added to the glaze. It seems vital, too, to add a stabilising oxide and this property is attributed to both red iron oxide and tin oxide. Between 1% and 2% of tin oxide is much in favour in modern recipes and Robert Tichane in his book, *Reds, Reds, Copper Reds* (see Bibliography), has put forward the explanation that it acts as a reducing agent. With such small amounts of colouring and opacifying oxide, it is not surprising that in an oxidised firing, copper red glazes are virtually colourless and indeed make bright, shiny transparent glazes in their own right.

Potters who fire copper reds often start reducing below 1000°C (1832°F) and maintain a reducing atmosphere through to the end of the firing. Some authorities say that a short period of oxidation at the end of the firing helps to brighten the colour. However, if you read the potter's notes alongside each recipe, there is certainly no consensus.

The overall reaction is explained by the black copper (cupric) oxide being reduced by oxygen-hungry carbon monoxide to produce copper metal and carbon dioxide:

$$CuO + CO > Cu + CO_2\char`\^$$

But this could also be explained by Robert Tichane's equation to explain the reducing power of tin oxide in the following steps:

1. The change from black to red (cuprous) copper oxide (Cu_2O) in reduction by carbon monoxide:
$$2CuO + CO > Cu_2O + CO_2\char`\^$$

Teapot by John Britt. Circular price stickers were used as a decoration to resist Pete's copper red glaze (COPR 1). These were peeled off and the round, bare areas painted with a black glaze.

2. The reduction of tin oxide to the monoxide form:
$$SnO_2 + CO > SnO + CO_2^\wedge$$
3. The cuprous oxide plus tin monoxide form copper metal and tin oxide:
$$Cu_2O + SnO > 2Cu + SnO_2$$

Above 1083°C (1981°F) metallic copper is in a molten state but as the glaze cools down the copper atoms can solidify. The red is sullied if applied over a buff stoneware and many potters use a white body to visually enhance the colour. The base glazes, too, are high in the alkaline fluxes K_2O and Na_2O, which improves the brightness of the colour response. This is often achieved by using little or no clay in the recipes and getting all the Al_2O_3 from the feldspar, thus maximising the amount of K_2O and Na_2O that can be brought into the glaze.

A good red colour will only develop if the glaze is fairly thick and will be colourless if applied too thinly. In some instances, these fluid glazes will slip down the pot, leaving a colourless white rim, gradually darkening towards the base.

COPR 1. Pete Pinnell's copper red, cone 9–10.

Potash feldspar	73.8
Gerstley borate	10.2
Whiting	11.1
Flint/quartz	4.9
	100.00
Tin oxide	1.0
Copper carbonate	0.3

% analysis of base glaze:
SiO_2 59.87; Al_2O_3 15.47; B_2O_3 3.00;
FeO 0.06; CaO 9.13; K_2O 9.84;
Na_2O 2.63

Potter's notes: This is Pete Pinnell's basic copper red, sometimes strawberry, glaze. Fired in reduction to cone 9–10 with a 10-minute period of oxidation at the end, and a natural cool.

COPR 2. Strawberry-purple glaze, cone 10 (from John Britt).

Potash feldspar	51.0
Ferro F3134	7.0
(a calcium borate frit)	
Barium carbonate	2.0
Lithium carbonate	2.0
Whiting	14.0
Zinc oxide	4.0
Flint/quartz	20.0
	100.0

Copper carbonate	0.6
Tin oxide	1.0

% analysis of base glaze:
SiO_2 57.73; Al_2O_3 9.58; B_2O_3 1.65; FeO 0.04; BaO 1.58; CaO 15.86; ZnO 4.07; K_2O 6.42; Na_2O 2.24; Li_2O 0.83

Potter's notes: Fired in reduction from cone 06 to cone 9, bending with a 10-minute oxidising soak. This glaze is shown on p.82.

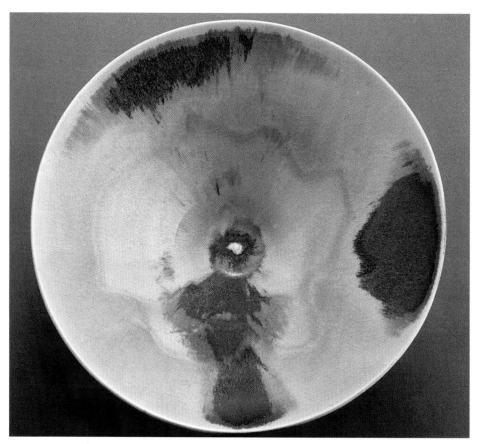

COPR 3. Porcelain bowl by John Britt.

COPR 4 on teapot by Melanie Brown. Note how the glaze's tendency to lose colour where thin accentuates the decoration.

COPR 3. Daiton Art Institute (DAI) copper red, cone 9–10.

Custer (potash) feldspar	48.2
Ferro F3134	9.1
(a calcium borate frit)	
China clay	5.5
Talc	3.6
Whiting	13.6
Zinc oxide	4.5
Flint/quartz	15.5
	100.0

Copper carbonate	0.9
Tin oxide	1.4

% analysis of base glaze:
SiO_2 60.35; Al_2O_3 11.94; B_2O_3 2.26; FeO 0.06; ZnO 4.84; CaO 10.37, MgO 1.24; K_2O 6.42; Na_2O 2.52

Potter's notes: Fired with moderate reduction from cone 08 to cone 10.

COPR 4. *Sang de Bouef, cone 10 (from Melanie Brown).*

Potash feldspar	32.0
Standard borax frit	11.0
China clay	20.0
Dolomite	11.0
Whiting	11.0
Flint/quartz	15.0
	100.0

Copper carbonate	0.5
Red iron oxide	0.5
Tin oxide	1.0

% analysis of base glaze:
SiO_2 58.03; Al_2O_3 16.78; B_2O_3 2.38; FeO 0.03, CaO 13.14; MgO, 2.77; K_2O 4.7; Na_2O 2.17

Potter's notes: I like this glaze on porcelain, and it is more exciting the hotter you fire it. Reduced from cone 05 to cone 10 bending.

COPR 5. *Copper red flambé, cone 10 (from Melanie Brown).*

Potash feldspar	34.0
Cornish stone	10.0
Standard borax frit	10.0
China clay	7.0
Bone ash	1.0
Whiting	18.0
Flint/quartz	20.0
	100.0

Copper carbonate	0.5
Red iron oxide	0.5
Rutile	1.0
Tin oxide	2.0

% analysis of base glaze:
SiO_2 63.49; TiO_2 0.01; P_2O_5 0.56; Al_2O_3 12.46; B_2O_3 2.07; FeO 0.04; CaO 13.66; MgO 0.02; K_2O 5.27; Na_2O 2.42

Potter's notes: The original glaze used colemanite which caused the glaze to throw itself off the pot. Adding borax frit as a substitute made the glaze more stable. Reduced from cone 05 to cone 10 bending.

COPR 6. *Classic oxblood, cone 9–10 (from Chris Prindl).*

FFF feldspar	73.0
Gerstley borate	10.0
Whiting	12.0
Flint	5.0
	100.0

Tin oxide	1.0
Copper carbonate	0.3

% analysis of base glaze:
SiO_2 60.78; P_2O_5 0.10; Al_2O_3 15.66; B_2O_3 2.96; FeO 0.06; CaO 10.06; K_2O 5.94; Na_2O 4.44

Potter's notes: I have found that the best substitute for 'ghastly' borate is BORAQ. As with all ox-bloods, this glaze must be thick to produce good colour but, if too thick, it can peel off. I have added modified cornstarch to help with adhesion. My favourite effect is a mixture of thin white areas, the deep red-black that forms next to the white, and the rest red. I reduce from cone 06 for 7 hours, keeping the reduction as strong as possible with a slow temperature rise until cone 9 is half over, then a final 40–60 minute oxidising soak.

COPR 7. *Copper red, cone 6+ (from Marcia Selsor).*

Nepheline syenite	55.3
Gerstley borate	12.6
Whiting	10.7
Flint/quartz	21.4
	100.0

Tin oxide	1.5
Copper carbonate	0.3
Red iron oxide	0.3

% analysis of base glaze:
SiO_2 62.63; Al_2O_3 14.85; B_2O_3 3.76; FeO 0.04; CaO 9.16; K_2O 3.01; Na_2O 6.55

Porcelain teapot by Melanie Brown using the flambé copper red COPR 5.

Potter's notes: Light reduction from cone 09 to cone 04, medium reduction to cone 6 with 45 minutes of heavier reduction at the end to even out the kiln. After shutting down, a few wooden sticks are introduced into the kiln; this is repeated two or three times hourly.

COPR 8. *Oxblood red, cone 9 (from Matthew Waite).*

Potash feldspar	78.7
High alkaline frit	9.1
Whiting	12.2
	100.0
Tin oxide	1.0
Copper oxide	0.4

% analysis of base glaze:
SiO_2 59.53; Al_2O_3 15.92; B_2O_3 0.38; FeO 0.07; CaO 8.05; K_2O 11.97; Na_2O 4.08

Thrown stool by Chris Prindl. The poured glaze COPR 6 shows the colour variations produced by glaze thickness.

COPR 7 on a mug by Marcia Selsor.

Copper red vase by Matthew Waite, using copper red (COPR 8) as an over-glaze.

Potter's notes: Finding this glaze was a bit of luck. The starting point was a Janice Tchalenko red over-glaze. The frit in the original recipe is calcium borate but I only had some high alkaline frit and tried that instead. Reduction starts at cone 07 and is maintained throughout the firing to cone 9.

COPR 9. *Copper red, cone 9–10 (from Paul Stubbs).*

Soda feldspar	45.0
Standard borax frit	15.0
China clay	5.0
Whiting	15.0
Quartz	20.0
	100.0
Copper carbonate	0.5
Tin oxide	2.0

% analysis of base glaze:
SiO_2 65.19; Al_2O_3 12.36; B_2O_3 3.05; FeO 0.07; CaO 12.33; K_2O 1.78; Na_2O 5.22

Wax-resist decoration over a satin-matt glaze (COPR 9) by Paul Stubbs.

Potter's notes: I use this as a double-dip or a trailed glaze over the satin-matt glaze ALU 2 (recipe on p. 57). This satin-matt glaze is receptive to the copper fumes coming from this copper red glaze.

COPR 10. *Copper red over-glaze, cone 9 (from Liz Gale).*

Potash feldspar	78.6
Standard borax frit	9.1
Whiting	12.3
	100.0

Copper carbonate	0.4
Tin oxide	1.0

% analysis of base glaze:
SiO_2 59.28; Al_2O_3 16.09; B_2O_3 1.8; FeO 0.07; CaO 9.07; MgO 0.01; K_2O 10.43; Na_2O 3.25

COPR 11. *Copper red, cone 9–10, used as an over-glaze (from David Frith).*

Potash feldspar	48.5
Petalite	4.9
Standard borax frit	6.8
Bentonite	1.0
Barium carbonate	1.9
Whiting	13.6
Zinc oxide	3.9
Quartz	19.4
	100.0

Copper carbonate	0.6
Tin oxide	1.0

% analysis of base glaze:
SiO_2 63.09; Al_2O_3 11.19; B_2O_3 1.37; FeO 0.11; ZnO 4.17; CaO 9.48; MgO 0.04; BaO 1.57; K_2O 6.57; Na_2O 2.15; Li_2O 0.26

Mirror by Liz Gale. COPR 10 and other coloured glazes trailed over a dark blue glaze, using Janice Tchalenko's recipes from *The Ceramic Review Book of Clay Bodies and Glaze Recipes* (1988).

Large vase (height: 50 cm/20 in.) by David Frith, using COPR 11, copper red over tenmoku.

Copper blues and greens

Although not having a well-known 'Oriental' pedigree, the next few glazes are used by reduction potters and serve to illustrate how different firings and base glazes can effect the final colour produced by copper.

COPB 1. Turquoise blue matt, cone 10 (from Douglas Phillips).

Nepheline syenite	59.0
Excelsior ball clay	1.5
(a high alumina ball clay)	
Barium carbonate	38.5
Lithium carbonate	1.0
	100.0

Copper oxide	3.0

% analysis of base glaze:
SiO_2 40.89; TiO_2 0.03; Al_2O_3 15.44; FeO 0.08; BaO 33.09; K_2O 3.31; Na_2O 6.71; Li_2O 0.45

Potter's notes: Take heed of health and safety notes when using barium carbonate. Only use on the outside of pots and no licking fingers!

COPB 2. *Turquoise barium blue matt, cone 9–10 (from John Harlow).*

FFF potash feldspar	55.6
Hymod AT ball clay	11.1
Barium carbonate	22.2
Whiting	11.1
	100.0

Copper carbonate	1.0
Cobalt carbonate	0.5
Titanium dioxide	2.0
Zirconium silicate	6.5

% analysis of base glaze:
SiO_2 48.72; TiO_2 0.15; P_2O_5 0.08; Al_2O_3 15.41; FeO 0.31; CaO 7.57; MgO 0.05; BaO 19.31; K_2O 5.08; Na_2O 3.23

Potter's notes: This works well both on its own and with the opal blue (JUN 4, p.65)

Turquoise blue matt (COPB 1) on a vase by Douglas Phillips.

Test tile from John Harlow showing COPB 2.

as an overlay, when very rich reds and blues can result – although this combination is very fluid and care must be taken to allow for glaze flow. The firing takes approximately 11 hours, reduction starts at 950°C (1742°F) until cone 9 is well over, and followed by a 20-minute oxidised soak.

COPB 3. Satin green, cone 9–10 (from John Harlow).

FFF potash feldspar	44.4
China clay	11.1
Ball clay	5.6
Barium carbonate	5.6
Whiting	22.2
Flint/quartz	11.1
	100.0

| Copper carbonate | 2.2 |
| Titanium dioxide | 8.9 |

% analysis of base glaze:
SiO_2 56.31; TiO_2 0.10; Al_2O_3 16.11; FeO 0.10; CaO 14.44; MgO 0.02; BaO 4.97; K_2O 6.45; Na_2O 1.50

Potter's notes: A peachy coloured variation of this glaze can be made by substituting 2.2% manganese dioxide for the copper carbonate.

COPB 4. Copper green opaque, cone 9–10 (from Glyn and Victor Harris).

Potash feldspar	47.0
China clay	8.0
Bentonite	1.0
Barium carbonate	21.0
Dolomite	4.0
Whiting	14.0
Flint/quartz	5.0
	100.0

Copper carbonate	2.5
Red iron oxide	1.5
C.M.C.	4.0

% analysis of base glaze:
SiO_2 46.85; Al_2O_3 13.61; FeO 0.15; CaO 10.79; MgO 1.05; BaO 18.91; K_2O 6.99; Na_2O 1.65

Potter's notes: This vase was once-fired, with the glaze mixed up thickly in a brush-on form. The firing is held around cone 09 to burn out the carbonates and with a heavy reduction from 930°C (1706°F) onwards until cone 10 bending. Our interest is to produce this green glaze in conjunction with a toasted reduction-fired body. A half-hour oxidising soak at the end of the firing allows the copper to re-oxidise (without this the glaze is a greyish pink!) although it is still subtly different to the glaze fired only in oxidation.

The copper red glazes COPR 1–11 and the copper blue satin and matt glazes COPB 1–4 are plotted on the graph (see p.109). This shows the copper red glazes grouped around the eutectic position, whilst the copper blues become increasingly matt as they move away from this area.

Large pot with COPB 3, satin-matt green, by John Harlow.

Redox firing (see Glossary) of COPB 4 on a bonsai planter by Glyn and Victor Harris.

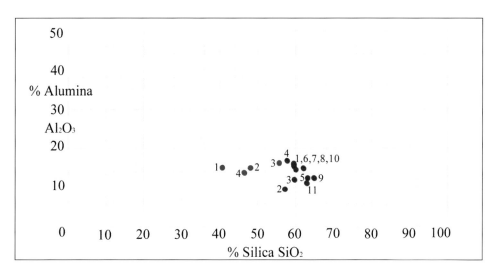

(**Fig. 12**) Graph plotting the distribution of the copper glazes. Copper reds = red spots. Copper blues = blue spots.

Chapter Eight
Plotting the raw materials

Another very useful aspect of plotting the silica:alumina percentage is that individual materials, as well as glazes, can be given a position on the graph. The graph below gives the position for some commonly used glaze ingredients, and can help in a pictorial way to explain how these materials will behave in glaze formation. Remember that the further we move away from the transparent area, in any direction, the more matte and opaque the glaze will become.

The possibilities for two ingredients

This looks at mixing whiting with both potash feldspar and Cornish stone. Without referring to the diagram could you say which one of these two recipes will make a transparent glaze when fired to cone 9?

Potash feldspar	85.0
Whiting	15.0
	100.0
Cornish stone	85.0
Whiting	15.0
	100.0

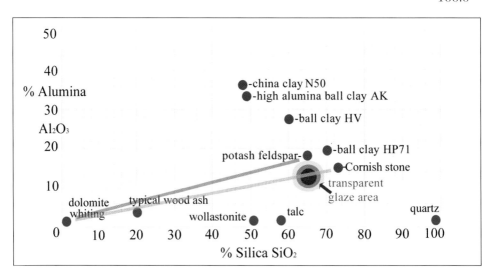

(**Fig. 13**) The SiO_2:Al_2O_3 positions for some glaze-making ingredients with the transparent cone 9 glaze area shown in red.
Blue line. A line blend between potash feldspar and whiting – missing the eutectic.
Green line. A line blend between Cornish stone and whiting – hitting the eutectic.

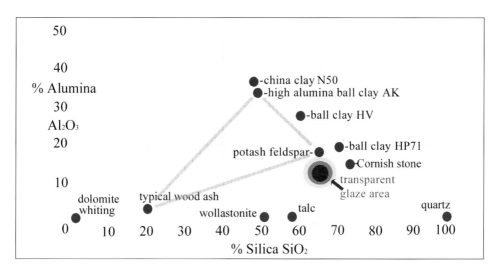

(Fig. 13a) The $SiO_2:Al_2O_3$ positions for some glaze-making ingredients with the transparent cone 9 glaze area shown in red. Glazes made from; wood ash, potash feldspar and AK ball clay would fall within the green triangle. Clearly these three ingredients are incapable of making a transparent glaze.

But, with the diagram to help (see Fig.13), the answer is a very easy one. A line blend between Cornish stone and whiting (shown in green) takes us through the eutectic position where transparent glazes are found (see TRA 2 on p.24). The potash feldspar/whiting line blend (shown in blue) would, by contrast, miss this area and thus be incapable of forming a transparent glaze at cone 9.

Can you read off any other potential transparent glaze-making combinations? The high silica ball clay called Hyplas71 and wollastonite looks a good bet, as does Cornish stone and wollastonite. Dolomite and china clay? No chance!

The possibilities for three ingredients

In Fig.13a three ingredients have been connected by a green line: wood ash, potash feldspar and an aluminous ball clay. These three ingredients could be used to make any glaze with an $SiO_2:Al_2O_3$ position falling within this triangle. We know from past experience (see Fig. 10 on p.70) that this encompasses the high alkaline and alumina glazes that we would call typical 'wood-ash' glazes. We can also say that, however hard we might try, it would be impossible for us to make a transparent cone 9 glaze by using just these ingredients alone.

Ideas for adjusting a glaze

This is an illustration of how to choose materials that will help to alter a glaze in a particular direction. For example, the Fig.13b shows Jim Robison's dry ash glaze ASH 4 (from p.48), plotted with a green dot at the SiO_2 46%:Al_2O_3 22% position. Now just suppose, for the sake of the argument, we wanted to make this less matt – what could we add?

Potash feldspar and Cornish stone look like good candidates to draw it away from the matt area and pull it towards, but not into, the transparent area. However, we could even hit the transparent

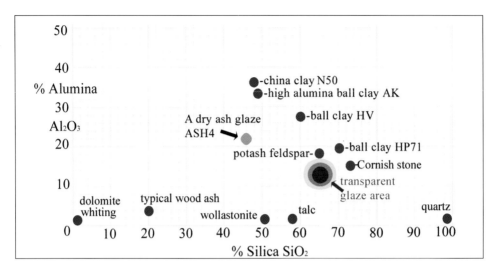

(Fig. 13b) The $SiO_2:Al_2O_3$ positions for some glaze-making ingredients, with the transparent cone 9 glaze area shown in red. Jim Robison's dry ash glaze ASH 4 is shown as a green dot. See text for ideas about how this glaze could be altered.

area by doing a line blend between ASH 4 and quartz!

Admittedly this doesn't tell us exactly how much to add, although measuring the distance between the ingredients (as with steps in a line blend) will give a good estimate.

And suppose an even drier glaze was required, we would have to go even further away from the transparent area. Extra china clay is a fairly obvious candidate, although we might also consider unbalancing it in other low SiO_2 directions by adding some more dolomite or whiting.

Chapter Nine
Glaze calculation and analysis

A basic requirement for the understanding of glazes is the ability to analyse a recipe in terms of its unity formula or percentage weight. Today we are very fortunate in having home computers that will do the number crunching for us, and the following list gives details about some well-known and useful programs. Potters will find that the 'answers', i.e. the analyses for particular glaze recipes, will vary slightly between these programs. This is not because any of them are getting their sums wrong! but because the programmers will have used marginally different analyses within their databases for the raw materials.

CeramDat and Glaze Workbook

David Hewitt's Pottery website gives information about his CeramDat program for MS Windows (and was used to do all the calculations in this book!). This is a stand-alone version of his spreadsheet-based Glaze Workbook. Some Mac users with MS Excel can also use this program. His site contains a number of technical articles and an extensive links page, including web links to all the addresses mentioned here. http://www.dhpot.demon.co.uk

GlazeBase

The San Diego State University data file called GlazeBase contains many glaze recipes and some downloadable programs for DOS and Macs, plus links to commercial software. It can be accessed through: http://art.sdsu.edu/ceramicsweb/glazesoftware.html

GlazeMaster

John Hesselberth has recently produced his GlazeMaster glaze program for use by both MS Windows and Mac users. The site refers to his work in connection with glaze stability and glazes for functional pottery. http://www.frogpondpottery.com

Insight

Tony Hanson's Digital Fire Corp. glaze calculation program, called Insight, is for MS Windows and Macs. The site contains an education section with numerous articles on a wide variety of pottery subjects. Select 'Glazes' and you will find a lot of useful information, much of which relates specifically to cone 9 glazes. http://www.digitalfire.com

The Matrix Glaze calculation program

Information about this comprehensive and versatile program can be found on Lawrence Ewing's website. Essentially MS Windows-based, the site also

contains very accessible analyses of over 700 raw materials.
http://www.Matrix2000.co.nz

The value of any glaze analysis depends upon having accurate data for the raw materials being used. A particularly useful site for the analyses and comparison of commercially available frits has been set up by Frank Gaydos and can be found at:
http://mysite.verizon.net/vze778gn/

Pyrometric cones

The Orton sites provides lots of useful information about pyrometry and can be found at:

http://www.ortonceramic.com
It includes a time/temperature equivalence chart (which can also be found in Appendix 6).

The Internet is a rapidly changing and expanding environment, and glaze calculation programs are no exception. Potters and organisations quite often change their website addresses, old sites shut down and new ones are added. Indeed the above list had to be updated while this book was in preparation, so there is no guarantee that some will not change again. However, the Internet search engines can be used to find hundreds of interesting sites under the headings of 'Pottery' and 'Ceramics'.

Appendix 1
Health and Safety

It would be impossible to list all the potential hazards associated with making and firing pottery. The following notes are not therefore offered as a definitive list but will hopefully indicate the main areas of concern.

Glazes and glazing

Although there may be differences in the labelling of ceramic materials from country to country, there is worldwide agreement that the following glaze ingredients can present a health risk:

Antimony oxide
Barium carbonate
Borax
Cadmium
Chromium oxide
Cobalt – carbonate and oxide
Copper – carbonate and oxide
Fluorine (a gas evolving from cryolite)
Lead
Lithium carbonate
Manganese – carbonate and dioxide
Nickel oxide
Selenium
Silver nitrate
Silica – flint and quartz
Vanadium pentoxide
Zinc oxide

For most materials the warning is related to 'excessive' use, but this can apply as much to a potter working for a lifetime in a small-scale craft workshop as it can to someone in an industrial situation. We should also be aware that people display a wide range of tolerance/ susceptibility to these materials. The Occupational Exposure Limits are quantified in relation to healthy adult males. Great care needs to be taken to ensure that children, pregnant women and nursing mothers avoid toxic materials. The main dangers will come from:
- Inhalation (fine dust and fumes)
- Ingestion (poisoning from toxic materials)
- Direct contact (irritation to eyes and skin)

Safety advice:
- Wear an approved particle filter mask when weighing out materials
- Work in a well-ventilated area
- Wear suitable, non-dust retentive clothing that is washed regularly. Keep the glaze-making area clean by wet washing. Spilt glazes need to be mopped up before they dry out. If vacuuming, only use an industrial vacuum cleaner designed for the job. Household vacuum cleaners must not be used as they fail to catch the finest, most hazardous silica particles. In fact, they create a greater danger by circulating them around the room.
- Do not drink, eat or smoke in the workshop
- Wash hands at the end of a work session

- Keep materials in closed containers
- If spraying glazes, use a spray booth and wear an appropriate mask
- Ensure that glazes used on functional ware are safe. If necessary, have them tested for solubility. The glaze should fit the body – crazed glazes lead to moisture absorption and a weakness in the structure of the work and are unhygienic

Kilns and firing

The main concerns here are:
- Electrocution
- Poisoning/suffocation
- Getting injured/burnt
- Setting fire to property

Safety advice:

For kilns in general:
- The kiln area needs to be very well ventilated; clays, glazes and fuel can give off toxic gases. If necessary use an extraction unit
- There should be at least 15 cm (6 in.) clearance around the kiln and sufficient space for servicing and repair.
- Wear a mask when handling ceramic fibre
- Allow the kiln to cool down before opening.
- Use gloves for unpacking the kiln
- Use eye protection, e.g. welder's goggles, against infrared radiation when looking into the kiln
- Ideally locate the kiln in a separate room
- An emergency procedure notice for shutting down the kiln should be prominently displayed
- A CO_2 fire extinguisher and a fire blanket should be kept in the kiln room
- Protect against contact with hot surfaces

- Keep a first aid kit on hand

Electric kilns:

- All electric kilns should be fitted with an automatic safety switch to cut off the electrical supply if the door is opened
- Do not totally rely on any automatic controller to turn the kiln off (check that it has done so)
- Check regularly for proper earthing and that all connections are secure and covered

Flame kilns:

- Firing flame kilns almost invariably means spending long periods of time around the kiln
- Keep the kiln area clean and tidy
- A particular concern is the creation of carbon monoxide during reduction firing (there are no respirators that protect against it). Adequate ventilation is vital
- Regularly check fuel lines – leaking fuels are potentially extremely dangerous and can accumulate into explosive mixtures
- Wear sensible clothing, footwear and gloves. Avoid synthetic fabrics which have a lower flashpoint than natural fibres
- If woodfiring, prepare fuel beforehand and stack to prevent excessive stooping
- Have water on hand for quenching draw trial and raking rods
- Organise comfortable accommodation and rest periods for long firings. Tiredness can lead to bad decisions being taken
- Clear away all combustible material from the kiln area at the end of the firing

Appendix 2
Glossary

Acidic oxides are classified as the non-metallic oxides that will react with water to form an acid. One property of acids is that they neutralise (and are neutralised by) basic and amphoteric substances, forming new compounds in the process. In our case, as glaze makers, these novel products are complex alumino-silicates, i.e. glasses, with heat needed to complete the reaction. By far the most important acidic oxide of the RO_2 group in stoneware glaze formation is silica (SiO_2).

Alkalis are the light metal, basic oxides of the R_2O group; lithia (Li_2O), soda (Na_2O) and potash (K_2O). They are very powerful fluxes and can be heated with silica to form glass (silicate).

Alkaline earths are also classed as basic oxides (RO group) with the most significant in high-temperature glaze chemistry being baria (BaO), calcia (CaO) and magnesia (MgO). Zinc oxide (ZnO) is actually a heavy metal, transition element but is usually classed as an 'honorary' alkaline earth as it behaves more like a basic oxide flux than a colouring metal oxide.

Alumina (Al_2O_3), in chemical terms is an intermediate (amphoteric) oxide capable of either behaving as an acid or an alkali. It acts as a stabiliser in the glass structure.

Amphoteric oxides are the R_2O_3 group of oxides intermediate between the basic and acidic oxides. In ceramics the most important is alumina.

Ball-mill is a revolving horizontal jar used for the tumble grinding of pottery materials. The volume of the jar is filled with approximately 25% grinding medium (pebbles or porcelain balls), 25% material for grinding, 25% water and 25% air.

Biscuit (bisque) firing is the first firing of unglazed ware; with the implication that a glaze-firing will follow.

Bloating occurs as blisters in the clay. It can be caused by carbonates and sulphates in the body not being burnt out properly or it may result from overfiring.

Body is a blend of clays.

Calcine is the driving-off of chemically combined carbon dioxide, CO_2, and water H_2O. This is useful, for example, if glazes or slips with a high clay content are to be applied to bisque ware.

Calcining some, or all of the clay in the recipe reduces its plasticity and stops the formation of cracks in the glaze or slip coat before firing. Potters can successfully calcine small quantities of glaze-making materials by heating in a small bowl in their normal bisque firing.

Clay is an extremely fine-grained, hydrated aluminium silicate. It is the fundamental material of ceramics.

Colouring oxides most commonly used in stoneware glazes are the metallic oxides of chrome, cobalt, copper, iron, manganese, nickel and vanadium.

Computer programs, in the context of this book, are programs that help the potter with the calculations involved in studying glazes.

Cone is a pyrometric device that deforms during firing, giving a measure of heatwork.

Crawling describes the defect wherein the glaze has pulled away from the clay in some places. The remaining glazed areas becomes drawn up and thickened.

Crazing occurs as fine cracks in the glaze. It is the result of the glaze being too tight a fit on the underlying clay body. It is generally regarded as a glaze defect, especially on functional tableware. However, when employed deliberately as a decorative technique, it may be described as 'crackle'.

Crystalline refers, in the firing of glazes, to the formation of crystals during cooling. The crystal structure 'grows' as a regular arrangement of atoms in a definite pattern. Thus they are solids within the glaze (a liquid).

Damper is a system which restricts the pull of the chimney, e.g. a plate that may be slid in, or across, the chimney to reduce the cross-sectional area.

Frit is a compound of glaze-forming chemicals that are melted together, cooled and then ground into a fine powder for use in a glaze. The main point, for stoneware potters, is that this allows soluble ingredients such as sodium oxide (Na_2O) and boric oxide (B_2O_3) to be used in an insoluble form in slop glazes. Minerals such as colemanite and gerstley borate are sometimes described as 'natural' frits.

Glazes are super-cooled liquids with the special property of being able to coat a clay body.

Glaze fit is a description of how compatible a glaze and the underlying clay are in terms of expansion and contraction after the firing. Unfortunately, problems such as crazing can take weeks, months or even years to show up.

Heatwork is a product of time and temperature. The advantage of pyrometric cones over electronic meters is that they give a measure of heatwork.

Line blending is a system which tests various combinations of two, three or four materials or mixtures. In glaze testing this is usually done by volume using a convenient measure such as a spoon.

Loss on Ignition (L.O.I.) is the percentage loss in weight of a material after heating.

Mineral is a naturally occurring chemical element or compound with a definite crystalline structure. Its chemical composition can be expressed as a formula, e.g. potash feldspar $K_2O.Al_2O_3.6SiO_2$.

Moisture crazing can result from the body absorbing moisture after firing. This causes the body to expand, forcing splits (craze lines) in the overlying glaze.

Molecule is a group of atoms bound by covalent bonds. The molecular formula gives the number of atoms within the molecule, e.g. a molecule of silica (SiO_2) contains one atom of silicon and two atoms of oxygen.

Once-fired is a glazing and firing method whereby the glaze is applied to the unfired body, and therefore only fired once. Also referred to as 'raw' glazing.

Opacifying oxides are those that remain in suspension within the glaze as it melts. Tin oxide and zirconium silicate are the two most frequently used white opacifiers. Glaze stains too are refractory and will remain in suspension. In a broader sense, though, other chemicals may be called 'opacifiers'. Titanium dioxide and zinc oxide, for example, can produce opaque crystals within the glaze as it cools down. Boric oxide and phosphorous pentoxide can form 'milky' hazes. Indeed almost any glaze material can be 'unbalanced' so that it overloads the glaze, causing opacity.

Oxidation is a chemical reaction that involves the addition of oxygen atoms. An oxidising atmosphere during firing is important, enabling carbonates and sulphates to be burnt out of the body. Oxidation is the opposite to reduction.

Percentage Analysis. Used in clay and glaze analysis to express the actual weight (in percent) of the oxides present in a material. The analysis of many materials will change when heated due to the loss on ignition and it is customary to present glazes in terms of their fired, rather than their un-fired, analyses.

Post-firing treatment refers to techniques that may be applied to the work after firing, e.g. staining crazed lines with coloured inks or using a small welding torch to 'torch in' or 'torch out' copper reds.

Primary air is the air mixed with the fuel before ignition.

Progression tests are used to explore the effect of adding one material to another. A typical example is the addition of a colouring metal oxide to a glaze in equal increments (a progression). This tests one variable in one direction.

Pyrometer is a device for measuring the temperature within the kiln.

Pyroxenes are a group of chain silicates, e.g. a calcium magnesium silicate $CaMgSi_2O_6$ called diopside. Such minerals tend to precipitate out of low alumina glazes, forming alkaline earth crystalline matts.

Quarl is the entry point for a burner flame.

Ratio is the numerical relationship of one thing to another. In this book, particular attention has been drawn to the relevance of the Al_2O_3:SiO_2 ratio in helping to understand the broad relationship between the various types of glaze.

Redox reaction is the alterations that result when changing from reducing to oxidising conditions (e.g. see the potter's notes about the COPB 4 copper glaze on p.106).

Reduction is a chemical reaction that involves the removal of oxygen atoms.

Refractory means capable of withstanding high temperatures.

Scattergrams are graphs that display pairs of linked data. The graphs used throughout this book have placed the scale for the value of the silica (SiO_2), component on the horizontal x-coordinate. The y-axis is used to represent the amount of alumina (Al_2O_3) in the glaze.

Secondary air is the air used in combustion which mixes with fuel after ignition.

Shivering is the opposite of crazing. With this defect the glaze is too big for the body. Slivers of the glaze spring away from the body, especially on edges such as handles and rims. The only good thing that can be said about shivering is that it usually happens within a day or two of the work coming out of the kiln. Even so, there are sorry tales about impecunious potters who have rushed out orders, literally hot from the kiln, only to be contacted the next day by puzzled shopkeepers asking for an explanation about the glaze 'falling' off the work!

Silica inversions are the two major reversible changes in the crystalline structure of free silica that take place during heating and cooling. They are:
- The cristobalite inversion, which takes place between 220°C (428°F) and 280°C (536°F), with any cristobalite expanding/contracting by 3% in volume
- The quartz inversion at 573°C (1063°F) with a +/−1% change in volume for any quartz present in the body or the glaze

Slop glaze is a mixture of fine glaze ingredients suspended in water.

Solubility is the ability of a substance to dissolve in a solution. This is particularly relevant in the 1. making, 2. firing and 3. functionality of glazes;
1. Slop glazes: where an excess of soluble materials causes a hard layer (cementation) to form in the bottom of the glaze tub. Under-fired frits are a particular problem for the studio potter.
2. Glaze melt: The action of heat brings about the formation of a liquid from the solids provided by the powders in the glaze recipe. In a perfect transparent glaze all of the oxides will have gone into solution. In matt and opaque glazes some of the oxides will not enter the melt but remain in suspension.
3. Acid attack of fired glazes: all functional pottery glazes should be able to withstand being attacked by the various acids associated with food and drink. The concern is that these acids may leach out poisonous metal compounds from the glazes and pass them on to the consumer. Low and under-fired glazes and glazes over-loaded with metal oxides present the greatest solubility hazard.

Solution is a liquid, e.g. water or liquid glaze, acting as a solvent and absorbing another substance (the solute). The solvent preserves its physical state and chemical structure.

Suspension is a mixture of fluid and solids, in which the particles do not dissolve and are inhibited from settling, e.g. ingredients in water as a slop glaze, or tin oxide in a molten glaze.

Temperature is a measure of heat. The two scales in common use by potters are the Centigrade (°C) and the Fahrenheit (°F) scales.

Unity Formula. This considers the material at the molecular level. The formula gives the ratio between the fluxes (totalling 1), the stabilisers and the glass formers.

Appendix 3

Typical percentage composition of raw materials used in this book.

FELDSPARS

	SiO_2	TiO_2	Al_2O_3	Fe_2O_3	P_2O_5	CaO	MgO	K_2O	Na_2O	L.O.I.
Cornish stone m.p.	73.20	0.06	15.30	0.13	0.47	1.47	0.13	4.45	3.44	1.35
Cornwall stone	71.10	0.50	16.80	0.16		1.60	0.05	6.57	2.29	0.93
Custer potash feldspar	68.50		17.50	0.08		0.30	0.01	10.40	3.00	0.21
FFF feldspar	67.90		19.00	0.10		1.00		7.00	5.00	0.00
Kona F4 soda feldspar	66.77		19.59	0.04		1.70	0.01	4.50	7.00	0.39
Nepheline syenite (1)	60.50		23.00	0.10		1.00		5.00	10.20	0.20
Nepheline syenite (2)	55.80		24.40	0.10		1.00		9.00	7.80	1.90
Potash feldspar	65.80		18.50	0.10		0.38		12.00	2.89	0.33
Soda feldspar	67.90		19.00	0.11		1.88		2.80	7.50	0.81

(1) = Lakeside, (2) = Northcape

CLAYS

	SiO_2	TiO_2	Al_2O_3	Fe_2O_3	P_2O_5	CaO	MgO	K_2O	Na_2O	L.O.I.
AK (TWVA)	49.20	0.09	33.70	1.20		0.20	0.30	1.50	0.10	13.71
Alberta slip	59.80		11.70	4.20		6.30	3.40	2.80	0.40	11.40
AT ball clay	54.00	1.10	29.00	2.40		0.30	0.40	3.00	0.50	9.30
Barnard slip	52.61	0.85	10.60	20.27		0.01	0.01	3.77		11.88
BB (BBV)	68.50	1.50	20.50	0.80		0.20	0.30	1.40	0.60	6.20
BLU (TWVD)	52.90	1.10	32.20	1.00		0.20	0.30	1.90	0.40	10.00
Calcined china clay	54.33	0.10	40.83	1.10		0.11	0.21	3.21	0.11	0.00
China clay N50	48.80	0.10	35.40	0.80				1.60	1.50	11.80
EPK kaolin	46.00	0.34	38.00	0.42		0.09	0.12	0.22	0.04	14.77
Excelsior	49.00	1.50	35.00	1.60		0.30	0.30	1.20	0.20	10.90
Grollegg china clay	48.00	0.02	37.00	0.70		0.06	0.30	1.85	0.10	11.97
Helmar kaolin	47.00		36.00	1.30		0.48	0.26	0.53	0.08	14.35
HP71 ball clay	70.00	1.60	19.00	0.80		0.20	0.40	2.00	0.50	5.50
HV (HVAR)	60.30	1.50	26.70	0.90		0.20	0.30	2.60	0.40	7.10
Molochite	53.00	0.08	44.00	1.00		0.10	0.10	1.60	0.12	0.00

Appendix 4

Typical percentage composition of materials used in this book.

MINERALS

	SiO$_2$	TiO$_2$	Al$_2$O$_3$	Fe$_2$O$_3$	P$_2$O$_5$	CaO	MgO	K$_2$O	Na$_2$O	Li$_2$O	L.O.I.
Barium carbonate (= 77.00% BaO)											
Bentonite	56.00		20.00	4.00		0.49	2.49	0.60	2.76		13.66
Bone ash					46.00	54.00					0.00
Dolomite	1.05		0.56	0.40		31.41	20.77	0.08	0.07		45.66
Flint	99.90		0.10								0.00
Kington stone	75.24	0.80	10.48	6.00	0.08	0.66	1.56	1.59	1.38		2.21
Lithium carbonate										40.00	60.00
Magnesium carbonate							48.00				52.00
Petalite	76.70		16.50	0.07		0.89	0.16	0.50	0.60	3.55	1.03
Quartz	99.90		0.10								0.00
Soda ash									58.50		41.50
Talc	58.30		0.15	0.22		0.42	33.40				7.51
Whiting	0.25					55.68	0.25				43.82
Wollastonite	51.40	0.03	0.50	0.76		46.20	0.25				0.86
Zinc oxide (= 100.00 % ZnO)										0.00	

WOOD ASHES

	SiO$_2$	Al$_2$O$_3$	Fe$_2$O$_3$	P$_2$O$_5$	CaO	MgO	K$_2$O	Na$_2$O	other
Pine ash	24.36	10.10	3.17	4.22	39.93	4.36	9.31	3.68	0.87
Willow ash	12.50		4.17	4.17	33.33	4.17	25.00	12.50	4.16
Wood ash generic	40.06	10.96	3.92	2.93	29.35	4.35	2.77	4.62	1.04

FRITS and other sources of boric oxide

	SiO$_2$	Al$_2$O$_3$	B$_2$O$_3$	CaO	MgO	BaO	K$_2$O	Na$_2$O	Li$_2$O
Calcium borate	17.90	4.90	50.30	26.50	0.10		0.30		
Colemanite	5.86	0.66	57.38	33.15	2.34		0.61		
F3110	69.88	3.53	2.69	6.24			2.17	15.49	
F3134	46.54		23.10	19.96				10.40	
Gerstley borate	27.60	9.14	34.86	24.61				3.79	
High alkaline	52.60	5.20	3.40	2.90		6.90	10.30	18.60	0.10
High temperature	65.80	6.70	15.30	3.70	3.10			5.40	
Standard borax	48.26	7.55	18.87	15.19	0.05		1.33	8.75	

Appendix 5

Calculations for using a synthetic wood ash.

Synthetic wood ash (from p. 46).

	%
Potash feldspar	5.0
Soda ash	5.0
High alkaline frit	17.0
Bone ash	8.0
Dolomite	15.0
Whiting	50.0
	100.0

This involves working out how much of the ingredients from the artificial recipe need to be substituted into the glaze recipe to make up the amount of wood ash. To find a certain % of anything you just move the decimal point to the left by two places and then multiply. For example to find; 1% you multiply by 0.01, to find 5% multiply by 0.05, to find 10% multiply by 0.1, to find 17% multiply by 0.17 and to find 50% multiply by 0.50 etc.

As an example here is the calculation to replace the wood ash in the famous 40:40: 20 Katherine Pleydell Bouverie recipe with the ingredients in the synthetic version.

Soda feldspar	40.0
Wood ash	40.0
Red clay	20.0
	100.0

The replacement of the 40 parts of wood ash may be calculated as follows.

Potash feldspar 5.0 % of 40
$$= 40 \times 0.05 = 2.0$$
Soda ash 5.0 % of 40 $= 40 \times 0.05 = 2.0$

High alk. frit 17.0 % of 40
$$= 40 \times 0.17 = 6.8$$
Bone ash 8.0 % of 40 $= 40 \times 0.08 = 3.2$
Dolomite 15.0 % of 40 $= 40 \times 0.15 = 6.0$
Whiting 50.0 % of 40 $= 40 \times 0.50 = 20.0$

Adding this into the recipe we get a synthetic 'wood ash' glaze.

Soda feldspar	40.0
Potash feldspar	2.0
Soda ash	2.0
High alkaline frit	6.8
Bone ash	3.2
Dolomite	6.0
Whiting	20.0
Red clay	20.0
	100.0

An alternative to doing these sums would be to make a large batch of the synthetic wood ash. The ingredients in the recipe from p.46 can be weighed out and then either dry or wet blended together. Dry blending (wear a mask) can be done by putting the ingredients in a suitable tub and stirring with an electric drill fitted with the type of attachment used for mixing plaster. Wet blending involves making the mixture into a slop glaze (as shown on p. 9) and then drying it out.

Of the two methods, wet blending probably gives a more thorough mix but is a far more laborious process and needs to be done in advance. In either way the required amount of 'wood ash' called for in a recipe can be taken out of this large batch without the need to do any calculations!

Appendix 6

Temperature equivalent chart for Orton pyrometric cones
Courtesy of the Edward Orton Jr Ceramic Foundation

Pyrometric cones have been used to monitor ceramic firings for more than 100 years. They are useful in determining when a firing is complete, if the kiln provided enough heat, if there was a temperature difference in the kiln or if a problem occurred during the firing.

Cones are made from carefully controlled compositions. They bend in a repeatable manner (over a relatively small temperature range – usually less than 5°C (40°F) The final bending position is an indication of how much heat was absorbed.

Typically it takes 15 to 25 minutes for a cone to bend once it starts. This also depends on the cone number. When the cone tip reaches a point level with the base, it is considered properly fired. However, cone bending may be affected by reducing atmospheres or those containing sulfour oxides. Orton recommend the use of iron-free cones for all reduction firings (cones 010–3).

If a cone is soaked at a temperature near its equivalent temperature, it will continue to mature and bend, soaking for 1 or 2 hours will deform the next cone up.

Bowl using oil-spot glaze (OIL 3) by John Britt.

Temperature Equivalent chart for Orton pyrometric cones (°C)

	Self Supporting Cones						Large Cones				Small
	Regular			Iron Free			Regular		Iron Free		Regular
	Heating Rate °C/hour (last 100°C of firing)										
Cone	15	60	150	15	60	150	60	150	60	150	300
022		586	590				N/A	N/A			630
021		600	617				N/A	N/A			643
020		626	638				N/A	N/A			666
019	656	678	695				676	693			723
018	686	715	734				712	732			752
017	705	738	763				736	761			784
016	742	772	796				769	794			825
015	750	791	818				788	816			843
014	757	807	838				807	836			870
013	807	837	861				837	859			880
012	843	861	882				858	880			900
011	857	875	894				873	892			915
010	891	903	915	871	886	893	898	913	884	891	919
09	907	920	930	899	919	928	917	928	917	926	955
08	922	942	956	924	946	957	942	954	945	955	983
07	962	976	987	953	971	982	973	985	970	980	1008
06	981	998	1013	969	991	998	995	1011	991	996	1023
05½	1004	1015	1025	990	1012	1021	1012	1023	1011	1020	1043
05	1021	1031	1044	1013	1037	1046	1030	1046	1032	1044	1062
04	1046	1063	1077	1043	1061	1069	1060	1070	1060	1067	1098
03	1071	1086	1104	1066	1088	1093	1086	1101	1087	1091	1131
02	1078	1102	1122	1084	1105	1115	1101	1120	1102	1113	1148
01	1093	1119	1138	1101	1123	1134	1117	1137	1122	1132	1178
1	1109	1137	1154	1119	1139	1148	1136	1154	1137	1146	1184
2	1112	1142	1164				1142	1162			1190
3	1115	1152	1170	1130	1154	1162	1152	1168	1151	1160	1196
4	1141	1162	1183				1160	1181			1209
5	1159	1186	1207				1184	1205			1221
5½	1167	1203	1225				N/A	N/A			N/A
6	1185	1222	1243				1220	1241			1255
7	1201	1239	1257				1237	1255			1264
8	1211	1249	1271				1247	1269			1300
9	1224	1260	1280				1257	1278			1317
10	1251	1285	1305				1282	1303			1330
11	1272	1294	1315				1293	1312			1336
12	1285	1306	1326				1304	1324			1355
13	1310	1331	1348				1321*	1346*			N/A
14	1351	1365	1384				1388*	1366*			N/A

Temperature Equivalent chart for Orton pyrometric cones (°F)

Cone	Self Supporting Cones Regular			Self Supporting Cones Iron Free			Large Cones Regular		Large Cones Iron Free		Small Regular
	27	108	270	27	108	270	108	270	108	270	540
022		1087	1094				N/A	N/A			1166
021		1112	1143				N/A	N/A			1189
020		1159	1180				N/A	N/A			1231
019	1213	1252	1283				1249	1279			1333
018	1267	1319	1353				1314	1350			1386
017	1301	1360	1405				1357	1402			1443
016	1368	1422	1465				1416	1461			1517
015	1382	1456	1504				1450	1501			1549
014	1395	1485	1540				1485	1537			1598
013	1485	1539	1582				1539	1578			1616
012	1549	1582	1620				1576	1616			1652
011	1575	1607	1641				1603	1638			1679
010	1636	1657	1679	1600	1627	1639	1648	1675	1623	1636	1686
09	1665	1688	1706	1650	1686	1702	1683	1702	1683	1699	1751
08	1692	1728	1753	1695	1735	1755	1728	1749	1733	1751	1801
07	1764	1789	1809	1747	1780	1800	1783	1805	1778	1796	1846
06	1798	1828	1855	1776	1816	1828	1823	1852	1816	1825	1873
05½	1839	1859	1877	1814	1854	1870	1854	1873	1852	1868	1909
05	1870	1888	1911	1855	1899	1915	1886	1915	1890	1911	1944
04	1915	1945	1971	1909	1942	1956	1940	1958	1940	1953	2008
03	1960	1987	2019	1951	1990	1999	1987	2014	1989	1996	2068
02	1972	2016	2052	1983	2021	2039	2014	2048	2016	2035	2098
01	1999	2046	2080	2014	2053	2073	2043	2079	2052	2070	2152
1	2028	2079	2109	2046	2082	2098	2077	2109	2079	2095	2163
2	2034	2088	2127				2088	2124			2174
3	2039	2106	2138	2066	2109	2124	2106	2134	2104	2120	2185
4	2086	2124	2161				2120	2158			2208
5	2118	2167	2205				2163	2201			2230
5½	2133	2197	2237				N/A	N/A			N/A
6	2165	2232	2269				2228	2266			2291
7	2194	2262	2295				2259	2291			2307
8	2212	2280	2320				2277	2316			2372
9	2235	2300	2336				2295	2332			2403
10	2284	2345	2381				2340	2377			2426
11	2322	2361	2399				2359	2394			2437
12	2345	2383	2419				2379	2415			2471
13*	2389	2428	2458				2410*	2455*			N/A
14*	2464	2489	2523				2530*	2491*			N/A

Heating Rate °F/hour (last 180°F of firing)

Bibliography

The following books are particularly recommended to potters and sculptors who require further reading on kiln building, reduction firing and glazes. They are divided into three sections, although there is inevitably some overlap.

General reference

Michael Cardew, *Pioneer Pottery*, A&C Black: American Ceramic Society, revised 2002.

Richard Dewar, *Stoneware*, A&C Black: University of Pennsylvania Press, 2002.

Frank & Janet Hamer, *The Potter's Dictionary of Materials and Techniques*, A&C Black, 5th ed. 2003.

Bernard Leach, *A Potter's Book*, Faber and Faber, 1940.

Daniel Rhodes, *Clay and Glazes for the Potter*, A&C Black: Krause Publications, reprinted 1998.

Kiln building and firing

Ian Gregory, *Kiln Building*, A&C Black, 2nd ed. 2001.

Nils Lou, *The Art of Firing*, A&C Black/ Gentle Breeze, 1998.

Coll Minogue & Robert Sanderson, *Wood-Fired Ceramics*, A&C Black/University of Pennsylvania Press, 2000.

Fred Olsen, *The Kiln Book*, A&C Black, 3rd ed.

Jack Tray, *Wood-Fired Stoneware and Porcelain*, Chilton, 1995.

Glazes

Michael Bailey, *Glazes Cone 6*, A&C Black, 2001.

Christine Constant & Steve Ogden, *The Potter's Palette*, Apple, 2000.

Emmanuel Cooper, *Clays and Glazes – the Ceramic Review Book of Clay Bodies and Glaze Recipes*, 3rd ed. 2001.

Ian Currie, *Stoneware Glazes: A Systematic Approach*, Bootstrap Press, 2nd. ed. 1989.

Greg Daly, *Glazes and Glazing Techniques*, A&C Black, 2nd ed. 1998.

Joseph Grebanier, *Chinese Stoneware Glazes*, Watson Guptill: Pitman Publishing, 1975.

Stephen Murfitt, *The Glaze Book*, Thames & Hudson, 2002.

Phil Rogers, *Ash Glazes*, A&C Black/ University of Pennsylvania Press, 2003.

Brian Sutherland, *Glazes from Natural Sources*, Batsford, 1987.

Robert Tichane, *Ash Glazes*, Krause Publications, 2nd ed. 1998.

Robert Tichane, *Celadon Blues*, Krause Publications, 2nd ed. 1998.

Robert Tichane, *Copper Reds*, Krause Publications, 1998.

Nigel Wood, *Chinese Glazes*, A&C Black/ University of Pennsylvania Press, 1999.

Nigel Wood, *Oriental Glazes, Their Chemistry, Origins and Re-creation*, Pitman Publishing, 1978.

Index